THE REVENGER'S TRAGEDY
CYRIL TOURNEUR

ISBN: 978-1502758309

Cover image: Alice Corrigan and Rachel Jane Carter in a production by SOOP Theatre. Copyright of Dan Finch.

[Dramatis Personae in order of appearance

VINDICI, the revenger, sometimes disguised as Piato

HIPPOLITO, his brother

GRATIANA, his mother

CASTIZA, his sister

DUKE

Two JUDGES

DUCHESS

LUSSURIOSO, the Duke's son by a previous marriage

AMBITIOSO, the eldest of the Duchess's three sons by a previous marriage

SPURIO, the Duke's bastard son

JUNIOR, the Duchess's youngest son

SUPERVACUO, the Duchess's middle son

ANTONIO, a virtuous old lord

PIERO, a virtuous lord

DONDOLO, Castiza's servant

LORDS

Two SERVANTS of Spurio

NOBLES

Four prison OFFICERS

A prison KEEPER

GENTLEMEN

NENCIO }

SORDIDO } Lussurioso's attendants

A FOURTH MAN in the final masque, Ambitioso's henchman

Guards]

I.i. [Outside Vindici's house]

Enter Vindici [with a skull]; the Duke, Duchess, Lussurioso [his] son, Spurio the bastard, with a train pass over the stage with torchlight.

VINDICI
Duke, royal lecher, go, gray-hair'd adultery;
And thou his son, as impious steep'd as he;
And thou his bastard, true-begot in evil;
And thou his duchess that will do with [the] devil:
Four ex'lent characters. Oh, that marrowless age
Would stuff the hollow bones with damn'd desires,
And stead of heat kindle infernal fires
Within the spendthrift veins of a dry duke,
A parch'd and juiceless luxur! Oh God, one
That has scarce blood enough to live upon!
And he to riot it like a son and heir?
Oh, the thought of that
Turns my abused heartstrings into fret!
Thou sallow picture of my poisoned love,
My study's ornament, thou shell of death,
Once the bright face of my betrothed lady,
When life and beauty naturally fill'd out
These ragged imperfections,
When two heaven-pointed diamonds were set
In those unsightly rings: then 'twas a face
So far beyond the artificial shine
Of any woman's bought complexion
That the uprightest man, if such there be,
That sin but seven times a day, broke custom
And made up eight with looking after her.
Oh, she was able to ha' made a usurer's son
Melt all his patrimony in a kiss,
And what his father fifty years told
To have consum'd, and yet his suit been cold!
But oh, accursed palace!
Thee, when thou wert apparel'd in thy flesh,
The old duke poison'd,
Because thy purer part would not consent
Unto his palsy-lust, for old men lustful
Do show like young men angry, eager-violent,
Outbid like their limited performances.
Oh, 'ware an old man hot and vicious!
"Age, as in gold, in lust is covetous."

Vengeance, thou murder's quit-rent, and whereby
Thou shouldst thyself tenant to tragedy,
Oh, keep thy day, hour, minute, I beseech,
For those thou hast determin'd! Hum: whoe'er knew
Murder unpaid? Faith, give revenge her due:
Sh'as kept touch hitherto. Be merry, merry;
Advance thee, O thou terror to fat folks,
To have their costly three-pil'd flesh worn of
As bare as this: for banquets, ease, and laughter
Can make great men, as greatness goes by clay,
But wise men little are more great than they.

Enter [his] brother Hippolito.

HIPPOLITO
Still sighing o'er death's vizard?

VINDICI
Brother, welcome;
What comfort bringst thou? How go things at court?

HIPPOLITO
In silk and silver, brother; never braver.

VINDICI
Puh,
Thou play'st upon my meaning. Prithee say,
Has that bald madam, opportunity,
Yet thought upon's? Speak, are we happy yet?
Thy wrongs and mine are for one scabbard fit.

HIPPOLITO
It may prove happiness.

VINDICI
What is't may prove?
Give me to taste.

HIPPOLITO
Give me your hearing then.
You know my place at court.

VINDICI
Ay, the duke's chamber.
But 'tis a marvel thou'rt not turn'd out yet!

HIPPOLITO
Faith, I have been shov'd at, but 'twas still my hap
To hold by th' duchess' skirt. You guess at that;
Whom such a coat keeps up can ne'er fall flat.
But to the purpose.
Last evening predecessor unto this,
The duke's son warily enquir'd for me,
Whose pleasure I attended: he began
By policy to open and unhusk me
About the time and common rumour;
But I had so much wit to keep my thoughts
Up in their built houses, yet afforded him
An idle satisfaction without danger.
But the whole aim and scope of his intent
Ended in this: conjuring me in private
To seek some strange-digested fellow forth
Of ill-contented nature, either disgrac'd
In former times, or by new grooms displac'd
Since his stepmother's nuptials, such a blood
A man that were for evil only good;
To give you the true word, some base-coin'd pander.

VINDICI
I reach you, for I know his heat is such:
Were there as many concubines as ladies
He would not be contain'd, he must fly out.
I wonder how ill-featur'd, vild-proportion'd
That one should be, if she were made for woman,
Whom at the insurrection of his lust
He would refuse for once. Heart, I think none,
Next to a skull, tho' more unsound than one:
Each face he meets he strongly dotes upon.

HIPPOLITO
Brother, y'ave truly spoke him.
He knows not you, but I'll swear you know him.

VINDICI
And therefore I'll put on that knave for once,
And be a right man then, a man a' th' time,

7

For to be honest is not to be i' th' world.
Brother, I'll be that strange-composed fellow.

HIPPOLITO
And I'll prefer you, brother.

VINDICI
Go to then;
The small'st advantage fattens wronged men,
It may point out. Occasion, if I meet her,
I'll hold her by the foretop fast enough,
Or like the French mole heave up hair and all.
I have a habit that will fit it quaintly.

[Enter Gratiana and Castiza.]

Here comes our mother.

HIPPOLITO
And sister.

VINDICI
We must coin.
Women are apt, you know, to take false money,
But I dare stake my soul for these two creatures,
Only excuse excepted that they'll swallow
Because their sex is easy in belief.

[GRATIANA]
What news from [court], son Carlo?

HIPPOLITO
Faith, Mother,
'Tis whisper'd there the duchess' youngest son
Has play'd a rape on Lord Antonio's wife.

[GRATIANA]
On that religious lady!

CASTIZA
Royal blood!
Monster, he deserves to die,
If Italy had no more hopes but he.

VINDICI
Sister, y'ave sentenc'd most direct and true:
The law's a woman, and would she were you.
Mother, I must take leave of you.

[GRATIANA]
Leave for what?

VINDICI
I intend speedy travel.

HIPPOLITO
That he does, madam.

[GRATIANA]
Speedy indeed!

VINDICI
For since my worthy father's funeral,
My life's unnatural to me, e'en compell'd
As if I liv'd now when I should be dead.

[GRATIANA]
Indeed he was a worthy gentleman,
Had his estate been fellow to his mind.

VINDICI
The duke did much deject him.

[GRATIANA]
Much?

VINDICI
Too much.
And through disgrace oft smother'd in his spirit
When it would mount, surely I think he died
Of discontent, the nobleman's consumption.

[GRATIANA]
Most sure he did!

VINDICI
Did he? 'Lack, you know all;
You were his midnight secretary.

[GRATIANA]
No.
He was too wise to trust me with his thoughts.

VINDICI
I'faith then, father, thou wast wise indeed:
"Wives are but made to go to bed and feed."
Come mother, sister; you'll bring me onward, brother?

HIPPOLITO
I will.

VINDICI
[*Aside to him*] I'll quickly turn into another.

Exeunt.

[I.ii. A court of law]

Enter the old Duke, Lussurioso his son, the Duchess, the Bastard, the Duchess' two sons Ambitioso and Supervacuo, the third her youngest brought out with Officers for the rape, two Judges.

DUKE
Duchess, it is your youngest son; we're sorry.
His violent act has e'en drawn blood of honour
And stain'd our honours,
Thrown ink upon the forehead of our state,
Which envious spirits will dip their pens into
After our death and blot us in our tombs,
For that which would seem treason in our lives
Is laughter when we're dead: who dares now whisper
That dares not then speak out, and e'en proclaim,
With loud words and broad pens our closest shame?

[FIRST] JUDGE
Your grace hath spoke like to your silver years
Full of confirmed gravity, for what is it to have
A flattering false insculption on a tomb,
And in men's hearts' reproach? The bowell'd corpse
May be cer'd in, but with free tongue I speak,
"The faults of great men through their [cerecloths] break."

DUKE
They do, we're sorry for't; it is our fate:
To live in fear and die to live in hate.
I leave him to your sentence; doom him, lords,
The fact is great, whilst I sit by and sigh.

DUCHESS
My gracious lord, I pray be merciful.
Although his trespass far exceed his years,
Think him to be your own as I am yours;
Call him not son-in-law. The law I fear
Will fall too soon upon his name and him;
Temper his fault with pity.

LUSSURIOSO
Good my lord,
Then 'twill not taste so bitter and unpleasant
Upon the judge's palate, for offenses
Gilt o'er with mercy show like fairest women,
Good only for their beauties, which wash'd of,
No sin is uglier.

AMBITIOSO
I beseech your grace,
Be soft and mild: let not relentless law,
Look with an iron forehead on our brother.

SPURIO
He yields small comfort yet; hope he shall die,
And if a bastard's wish might stand in force,
Would all the court were turn'd into a corse.

DUCHESS
No pity yet? Must I rise fruitless then?
A wonder in a woman. Are my knees
Of such low metal that without respect--

FIRST JUDGE
Let the offender stand forth.
'Tis the duke's pleasure that impartial doom
Shall take [fast] hold of his unclean attempt.
A rape! Why, 'tis the very core of lust,
Double adultery!

JUNIOR
So, sir.

SECOND JUDGE
And which was worse,
Committed on the Lord Antonio's wife,
That general honest lady. Confess, my lord!
What mov'd you to't?

JUNIOR
Why, flesh and blood, my lord.
What should move men unto a woman else?

LUSSURIOSO
Oh, do not jest thy doom; trust not an axe
Or sword too far: the law is a wise serpent
And quickly can beguile thee of thy life.
Tho' marriage only has [made] thee my brother,
I love thee so far; play not with thy death.

JUNIOR
I thank you, troth; good admonitions, faith,
If I'd the grace now to make use of them.

FIRST JUDGE
That lady's name has spread such a fair wing
Over all Italy, that if our tongues
Were sparing toward the fact, judgment itself
Would be condemned and suffer in men's thoughts.

JUNIOR
Well then, 'tis done, and it would please me well
Were it to do again: sure [she's] a goddess,
For I'd no power to see her and to live.
It falls out true in this, for I must die:
Her beauty was ordain'd to be my scaffold.
And yet [methinks] I might be easier [cess'd],
My fault being sport, let me but die in jest.

FIRST JUDGE
This be the sentence.

DUCHESS
Oh, keep 't upon your tongue; let it not slip:

Death too soon steals out of a lawyer's lip.
Be not so cruel-wise.

FIRST JUDGE
Your grace must pardon us;
'Tis but the justice of the law.

DUCHESS
The law
Is grown more subtle than a woman should be.

SPURIO
[*Aside*] Now, now he dies; rid 'em away.

DUCHESS
[*Aside*] Oh, what it is to have an old, cool duke,
To be as slack in tongue as in performance!

FIRST JUDGE
Confirm'd; this be the doom irrevocable.

DUCHESS
Oh!

FIRST JUDGE
Tomorrow early--

DUCHESS
Pray be a-bed, my lord.

FIRST JUDGE
Your grace much wrongs yourself.

AMBITIOSO
No, 'tis that tongue,
Your too much right, does do us too much wrong.

FIRST JUDGE
Let that offender--

DUCHESS
Live, and be in health.

FIRST JUDGE
Be on a scaffold--

DUKE
Hold, hold, my lord.

SPURIO
[*Aside*] Pax on't,
What makes my dad speak now?

DUKE
We will defer the judgment till next sitting.
In the meantime let him be kept close prisoner:
Guard, bear him hence.

[Ambitioso and Supervacuo take Junior aside.]

AMBITIOSO
Brother, this makes for thee;
Fear not, we'll have a trick to set thee free.

JUNIOR
Brother, I will expect it from you both,
And in that hope I rest.

SUPERVACUO
Farewell, be merry.

Exit [Junior] with a guard.

SPURIO
[*Aside*] Delay'd, deferr'd! Nay, then if judgment have cold blood,
Flattery and bribes will kill it.

DUKE
About it then, my lords, with your best powers;
More serious business calls upon our hours.

Exeunt [omnes]. Manet Duchess.

DUCHESS
Wast ever known step-duchess was so mild
And calm as I? Some now would plot his death
With easy doctors, those loose-living men,
And make his wither'd grace fall to his grave
And keep church better.
Some second wife would do this, and dispatch
Her double-loath'd lord at meat and sleep.

Indeed, 'tis true an old man's twice a child.
Mine cannot speak; one of his single words
Would quite have freed my youngest, dearest son
From death or durance, and have made him walk
With a bold foot upon the thorny law,
Whose prickles should bow under him: but 'tis not,
And therefore wedlock, faith, shall be forgot.
I'll kill him in his forehead; hate there feed:
That wound is deepest tho' it never bleed.

[Enter Spurio.]

[Aside] And here comes he whom my heart points unto,
His bastard son, but my love's true-begot.
Many a wealthy letter have I sent him,
Swell'd up with jewels, and the timorous man
Is yet but coldly kind;
That jewel's mine that quivers in his ear,
Mocking his master's chillness and vain fear.
H'as spied me now.

SPURIO
Madam? Your grace so private?
My duty on your hand.

[He kisses her hand.]

DUCHESS
Upon my hand, sir! Troth, I think you'd fear
To kiss my hand too if my lip stood there.

SPURIO
Witness I would not, madam.

DUCHESS
Tis a wonder,
For ceremony [has] made many fools.
It is as easy way unto a duchess
As to a hatted dame, if her love answer,
But that by timorous honours, pale respects,
Idle degrees of fear, men make their ways
Hard of themselves. What have you thought of me?

SPURIO
Madam, I ever think of you in duty,
Regard, and--

DUCHESS
Puh, upon my love, I mean!

SPURIO
I would 'twere love, but ['t 'as] a fouler name
Than lust; you are my father's wife: your grace may guess now
What I could call it.

DUCHESS
Why, th'art his son but falsely;
'Tis a hard question whether he begot thee.

SPURIO
I'faith, 'tis true too; I'm an uncertain man,
Of more uncertain woman. Maybe his groom
A' th' stable begot me; you know I know not.
He could ride a horse well; a shrewd suspicion, marry!
He was wondrous tall; he had his length, i'faith,
For peeping over half shut holy-day windows:
Men would desire him light! When he was afoot,
He made a goodly show under a penthouse,
And when he rid, his hat would check the signs
And clatter barbers' basins.

DUCHESS
Nay, set you a-horseback once,
You'll ne'er light off.

SPURIO
Indeed, I am a beggar.

DUCHESS
That's more the sign thou art great. But to our love:
Let it stand firm both in thought and mind.
That the duke was thy father, as no doubt then
He bid fair for't, thy injury is the more,
For had he cut thee a right diamond,
Thou hadst been next set in the dukedom's ring
When his worn self like age's easy slave
Had dropp'd out of the collet into th' grave.

What wrong can equal this? Canst thou be tame
And think upon't?

SPURIO
No, mad and think upon't!

DUCHESS
Who would not be reveng'd of such a father,
E'en in the worst way? I would thank that sin
That could most injury him and be in league with it.
Oh, what a grief 'tis, that a man should live
But once i' th' world, and then to live a bastard,
The curse a' the womb, the thief of nature,
Begot against the seventh commandment,
Half-damn'd in the conception, by the justice
Of that unbribed, everlasting law!

SPURIO
Oh, I'd a hot-back'd devil to my father!

DUCHESS
Would not this mad e'en patience, make blood rough?
Who but an eunuch would not sin, his bed
By one false minute disinherited?

SPURIO
Ay, there's the vengeance that my birth was wrapp'd in;
I'll be reveng'd for all. Now hate begin;
I'll call foul incest but a venial sin.

DUCHESS
Cold still? In vain then must a duchess woo?

SPURIO
Madam, I blush to say what I will do.

DUCHESS
Thence flew sweet comfort, earnest and farewell.

[She kisses him.]

SPURIO
Oh, one incestuous kiss picks open hell!

DUCHESS
[*Aside*] Faith, now, old duke, my vengeance shall reach high;
I'll arm thy brow with woman's heraldry.

Exit.

SPURIO
Duke, thou didst do me wrong, and by thy act
Adultery is my nature.
Faith, if the truth were known, I was begot
After some gluttonous dinner; some stirring dish
Was my first father. When deep healths went round,
And ladies' cheeks were painted red with wine,
Their tongues as short and nimble as their heels,
Uttering words sweet and thick, and when they [rose]
Were merrily dispos'd to fall again:
In such a whisp'ring and withdrawing hour,
When base male-bawds kept sentinel at stair-head,
Was I stol'n softly. Oh, damnation met
The sin of feasts, drunken adultery!
I feel it swell me; my revenge is just:
I was begot in impudent wine and lust.
Stepmother, I consent to thy desires;
I love thy mischief well, but I hate thee
And those three cubs, thy sons, wishing confusion,
Death, and disgrace may be their epitaphs.
As for my brother, the duke's only son,
Whose birth is more beholding to report
Than mine, and yet perhaps as falsely sown--
Women must not be trusted with their own--
I'll loose my days upon him: hate all I.
Duke, on thy brow I'll draw my bastardy,
For indeed a bastard by nature should make cuckolds,
Because he is the son of a cuckold-maker.

Exit.

[I.iii. The palace]

Enter Vindici and Hippolito, Vindici in disguise [as Piato] to attend Lord Lussurioso, the duke's son.

VINDICI
What, brother? Am I far enough from myself?

HIPPOLITO
As if another man had been sent
Into the world, and none wist how he came.

VINDICI
It will confirm me bold, the child a' th' court:
Let blushes dwell i' th' country. Impudence,
Thou goddess of the palace, [mistress] of [mistresses]
To whom the costly-perfum'd people pray,
Strike thou my forehead into dauntless marble,
Mine eyes to steady sapphires: turn my visage,
And if I must needs glow, let me blush inward
That this immodest season may not spy
That scholar in my cheeks, fool-bashfulness,
That maid in the old time, whose flush of grace
Would never suffer her to get good clothes.
Our maids are wiser and are less asham'd;
Save grace the bawd I seldom hear grace nam'd!

HIPPOLITO
Nay, brother, you reach out a' th' verge now.

[Enter Lussurioso.]

'Sfoot, the duke's son! Settle your looks.

VINDICI
Pray let me not be doubted.

HIPPOLITO
My lord--

LUSSURIOSO
Hippolito? Be absent; leave us.

HIPPOLITO
My lord, after long search, wary inquiries
And politic siftings, I made choice of yon fellow,
Whom I guess rare for many deep employments;
This our age swims within him: and if Time
Had so much hair, I should take him for Time,
He is so near kin to this present minute.

LUSSURIOSO
'Tis enough;
We thank thee. Yet words are but great men's blanks:
Gold, tho' it be dumb, does utter the best thanks.

[He gives Hippolito gold.]

HIPPOLITO
Your plenteous honour; an ex'lent fellow, my lord.

LUSSURIOSO
So, give us leave.

Exit [Hippolito].

Welcome, be not far off, we must be better acquainted. Push, be bold with us,
thy hand!

VINDICI
With all my heart, i'faith. How dost, sweet musk-cat?
When shall we lie together?

LUSSURIOSO
[Aside] Wondrous knave!
Gather him into boldness? 'Sfoot, the slave's
Already as familiar as an ague,
And shakes me at his pleasure!--Friend, I can
Forget myself in private, but elsewhere,
I pray do you remember me.

VINDICI
Oh, very well, sir.
I conster myself saucy.

LUSSURIOSO
What hast been?
Of what profession?

VINDICI
A bone-setter.

LUSSURIOSO
A bone-setter!

VINDICI
A bawd, my lord,
One that sets bones together.

LUSSURIOSO
[*Aside*] Notable bluntness!
Fit, fit for me, e'en train'd up to my hand.--
Thou hast been scrivener to much knavery then?

VINDICI
Fool to abundance, sir. I have been witness
To the surrenders of a thousand virgins,
And not so little;
I have seen patrimonies wash'd a' pieces,
Fruit-fields turn'd into bastards,
And in a world of acres,
Not so much dust due to the heir 'twas left to
As would well gravel a petition!

LUSSURIOSO
[*Aside*] Fine villain! Troth, I like him wondrously.
He's e'en shap'd for my purpose.--Then thou know'st
I' th' world strange lust.

VINDICI
Oh, Dutch lust! Fulsome lust!
Drunken procreation, which begets
So many drunkards! Some father dreads not, gone
To bed in wine, to slide from the mother
And cling the daughter-in-law,
Some uncles are adulterous with their nieces,
Brothers with brothers' wives. Oh, hour of incest!
Any kin now next to the rim a' th' sister
Is man's meat in these days, and in the morning
When they are up and dress'd, and their mask on,
Who can perceive this save that eternal eye
That sees through flesh and all well. If anything be damn'd,
It will be twelve a' clock at night; that twelve
Will never 'scape:
It is the Judas of the hours, wherein
Honest salvation is betray'd to sin.

LUSSURIOSO
In troth, it is too; but let this talk glide.

It is our blood to err, tho' hell gap'd loud:
Ladies know Lucifer fell, yet still are proud.
Now, sir. Wert thou as secret as thou'rt subtle,
And deeply fadom'd into all estates,
I would embrace thee for a near employment,
And thou shouldst swell in money, and be able
To make lame beggars crouch to thee.

VINDICI
My lord?
Secret? I ne'er had that disease a' th' mother,
I praise my father: why are men made close,
But to keep thoughts in best? I grant you this,
Tell but some woman a secret overnight,
Your doctor may find it in the urinal i' th' morning.
But, my lord--

LUSSURIOSO
So, thou'rt confirmed in me,
And thus I enter thee.

VINDICI
This Indian devil
Will quickly enter any man but a usurer;
He prevents that by ent'ring the devil first.

LUSSURIOSO
Attend me: I am past my [depth] in lust
And I must swim or drown; all my desires
Are level'd at a virgin not far from court,
To whom I have convey'd by messenger
Many wax'd lines, full of my neatest spirit,
And jewels that were able to ravish her
Without the help of man, all which and more
She, foolish-chaste, sent back, the messengers
Receiving frowns for answers.

VINDICI
Possible?
'Tis a rare phoenix, whoe'er she be,
If your desires be such, she so repugnant.
In troth, my lord, I'd be reveng'd and marry her.

LUSSURIOSO
Push, the dowry of her blood and of her fortunes
Are both too mean, good enough to be bad withal.
I'm one of that number can defend
Marriage is good, yet rather keep a friend.
Give me my bed by stealth; there's true delight:
What breeds a loathing in't but night by night?

VINDICI
A very fine religion!

LUSSURIOSO
Therefore thus:
I'll trust thee in the business of my heart
Because I see thee well experienc'd
In this luxurious day wherein we breathe.
Go thou, and with a smooth, enchanting tongue
Bewitch her ears and cozen her of all grace.
Enter upon the portion of her soul,
Her honour, which she calls her chastity,
And bring it into expense, for honesty
Is like a stock of money laid to sleep,
Which ne'er so little broke does never keep.

VINDICI
You have gi'n 't the tang, i'faith, my lord.
Make known the lady to me, and my brain
Shall swell with strange invention: I will move it
Till I expire with speaking, and drop down
Without a word to save me; but I'll work.

LUSSURIOSO
We thank thee, and will raise thee: receive her name;
It is the only daughter to Madam Gratiana,
The late widow.

VINDICI
[Aside] Oh, my sister, my sister!

LUSSURIOSO
Why dost walk aside?

VINDICI
My lord, I was thinking how I might begin,

As thus, "Oh, lady," or twenty hundred devices;
Her very bodkin will put a man in.

LUSSURIOSO
Ay, or the wagging of her hair.

VINDICI
No, that shall put you in, my lord.

LUSSURIOSO
Shall 't? Why, content. Dost know the daughter then?

VINDICI
Oh, ex'lent well by sight.

LUSSURIOSO
That was her brother
That did prefer thee to us.

VINDICI
My lord, I think so;
I knew I had seen him somewhere.

LUSSURIOSO
And therefore, prithee, let thy heart to him
Be as a virgin, close.

VINDICI
Oh, [my] good lord!

LUSSURIOSO
We may laugh at that simple age within him.

VINDICI
Ha, ha, ha!

LUSSURIOSO
Himself being made the subtle instrument
To wind up a good fellow.

VINDICI
That's I, my lord.

LUSSURIOSO
That's thou,
To entice and work his sister.

VINDICI
A pure novice!

LUSSURIOSO
'Twas finely manag'd.

VINDICI
Gallantly carried.
[*Aside*] A pretty, perfum'd villain!

LUSSURIOSO
I've bethought me,
If she prove chaste still and immoveable,
Venture upon the mother, and with gifts
As I will furnish thee, begin with her.

VINDICI
Oh, fie, fie, that's the wrong end, my lord! 'Tis mere impossible that a mother
by any gifts should become a bawd to her own daughter!

LUSSURIOSO
Nay, then I see thou'rt but a puny in the subtle mystery of a woman.
Why, 'tis held now no dainty dish: the name
Is so in league with age that nowadays
It does eclipse three quarters of a mother.

VINDICI
Dost so, my lord?
Let me alone then to eclipse the fourth.

LUSSURIOSO
Why, well said; come, I'll furnish thee, but first
Swear to be true in all.

VINDICI
True?

LUSSURIOSO
Nay, but swear!

VINDICI
Swear?
I hope your honour little doubts my faith.

LUSSURIOSO
Yet for my humour's sake, 'cause I love swearing.

VINDICI
'Cause you love swearing, 'slud, I will.

LUSSURIOSO
Why, enough,
Ere long look to be made of better stuff.

VINDICI
That will do well indeed, my lord.

LUSSURIOSO
Attend me.

Exit.

VINDICI
Oh,
Now let me burst: I've eaten noble poison!
We are made strange fellows, brother, innocent villains.
Wilt not be angry when thou hear'st on't, think'st thou?
I'faith, thou shalt; swear me to foul my sister!
Sword, I durst make a promise of him to thee,
Thou shalt dis-heir him, it shall be thine honour!
And yet now angry froth is down in me,
It would not prove the meanest policy
In this disguise to try the faith of both;
Another might have had the selfsame office,
Some slave that would have wrought effectually,
Ay, and perhaps o'erwrought 'em. Therefore I,
Being thought travell'd, will apply myself
Unto the selfsame form, forget my nature,
As if no part about me were kin to 'em;
So touch 'em, tho' I durst almost for good
Venture my lands in heaven upon their [blood].

Exit.

[I.iv. Antonio's house]

*Enter the discontented Lord Antonio, whose wife the Duchess' youngest son ravish'd,
he discovering the body of her dead to [Piero and other] certain Lords and Hippolito.*

ANTONIO
Draw nearer, lords, and be sad witnesses
Of a fair, comely building newly fall'n,
Being falsely undermined: violent rape
Has play'd a glorious act. Behold, my lords,
A sight that strikes man out of me.

PIERO
That virtuous lady?

ANTONIO
President for wives!

HIPPOLITO
The blush of many women, whose chaste presence
Would e'en call shame up to their cheeks,
And make pale wanton sinners have good colours--

ANTONIO
Dead!
Her honour first drunk poison, and her life,
Being fellows in one house, did pledge her honour.

PIERO
Oh, grief of many!

ANTONIO
I mark'd not this before.
A prayer book the pillow to her cheek,
This was her rich confection, and another
Plac'd in her right hand, with a leaf tuck'd up,
Pointing to these words:
"Melius virtute mori, quam per dedecus vivere."
True and effectual it is indeed.

HIPPOLITO
My lord, since you invite us to your sorrows,
Let's truly taste 'em, that with equal comfort
As to ourselves we may relieve your wrongs;

We have grief too that yet walks without tongue:
Curae leves loquuntur, majores stupent.

ANTONIO
You deal with truth, my lord.
Lend me but your attentions, and I'll cut
Long grief into short words: last revelling night,
When torch-light made an artificial noon
About the court, some courtiers in the masque,
Putting on better faces than their own,
Being full of fraud and flattery, amongst whom
The duchess' youngest son, that moth to honour,
Fill'd up a room, and with long lust to eat
Into my wearing, amongst all the ladies,
Singled out that dear form, who ever liv'd
As cold in lust as she is now in death,
Which that step-duchess' monster knew too well;
And therefore in the height of all the revels,
When music was hard loudest, courtiers busiest,
And ladies great with laughter. Oh, vicious minute!
Unfit but for relation to be spoke of!
Then with a face more impudent than his vizard,
He harried her amidst a throng of panders,
That live upon damnation of both kinds,
And fed the ravenous vulture of his lust!
Oh, death to think on't! She, her honour forc'd,
Deem'd it a nobler dowry for her name
To die with poison than to live with shame.

HIPPOLITO
A wondrous lady; of rare fire compact:
Sh'as made her name an empress by that act.

PIERO
My lord, what judgment follows the offender?

ANTONIO
Faith, none, my lord: it cools and is deferr'd.

PIERO
Delay the doom for rape?

ANTONIO
Oh, you must note who 'tis should die:

The Duchess' son; she'll look to be a saver.
"Judgment in this age is ne'er kin to favour."

HIPPOLITO
[*Drawing his sword*] Nay, then step forth, thou bribeless officer.
I bind you all in steel to bind you surely:
Here let your oaths meet to be kept and paid,
Which else will stick like rust and shame the blade.
Strengthen my vow, that if at the next sitting
Judgment speak all in gold, and spare the blood
Of such a serpent, e'en before their seats,
To let his soul out, which long since was found
Guilty in heaven.

ALL [LORDS]
We swear it and will act it.

ANTONIO
Kind gentlemen, I thank you in mine ire.

HIPPOLITO
'Twere pity
The ruins of so fair a monument
Should not be dipp'd in the defacer's blood.

PIERO
Her funeral shall be wealthy, for her name
Merits a tomb of pearl. My Lord Antonio,
For this time wipe your lady from your eyes;
No doubt our grief and yours may one day court it,
When we are more familiar with revenge.

ANTONIO
That is my comfort, gentlemen, and I joy
In this one happiness above the rest,
Which will be call'd a miracle at last,
That being an old man I'd a wife so chaste.

Exeunt.

II.i. [Vindici's house]

Enter Castiza the sister.

CASTIZA

How hardly shall that maiden be beset
Whose only fortunes are her constant thoughts,
That has no other child's part but her honour
That keeps her low and empty in estate.
Maids and their honours are like poor beginners:
Were not sin rich there would be fewer sinners.
Why had not virtue a revenue? Well,
I know the cause: 'twould have impoverish'd hell.

Enter Dondolo.

How now, Dondolo?

DONDOLO

[Madonna], there is one, as they say, a thing of flesh and blood, a man I take
him by his beard, that would very desirously mouth to mouth with you.

CASTIZA

What's that?

DONDOLO

Show his teeth in your company.

CASTIZA

I understand thee not.

DONDOLO

Why, speak with you, Madonna!

CASTIZA

Why, say so, madman, and cut of a great deal of dirty way. Had it not been
better spoke in ordinary words that one would speak with me?

DONDOLO

Ha, ha, that's as ordinary as two shillings! I would strive a little to show myself
in my place: a gentleman usher scorns to use the phrase and fancy of a
serving-man.

CASTIZA

Yours be your [own], sir; go direct him hither.

[Exit Dondolo.]

I hope some happy tidings from my brother
That lately travell'd, whom my soul affects.

Enter [Vindici] her brother disguised [as Piato].

Here he comes.

VINDICI
[*Giving her a jewel*] Lady, the best of wishes to your sex,
Fair skins and new gowns.

CASTIZA
Oh, they shall thank you, sir.
Whence this?

VINDICI
Oh, from a dear and worthy friend, mighty!

CASTIZA
From whom?

VINDICI
The duke's son!

CASTIZA
Receive that!

A box a' th' ear to her brother.

I swore I'd put anger in my hand
And pass the virgin limits of myself
To him that next appear'd in that base office
To be his sin's attorney; bear to him
That figure of my hate upon thy cheek
Whilst 'tis yet hot, and I'll reward thee for't.
Tell him my honour shall have a rich name
When several harlots shall share his with shame.
Farewell; commend me to him in my hate!

Exit.

VINDICI
It is the sweetest box
That e'er my nose came nigh,
The finest drawn-work cuff that e'er was worn.

I'll love this blow forever, and this cheek
Shall still hence forward take the wall of this.
Oh, I'm above my tongue! Most constant sister,
In this thou hast right honourable shown;
Many are call'd by their honour that have none.
Thou art approv'd forever in my thoughts.
It is not in the power of words to taint thee,
And yet for the salvation of my oath,
As my resolve in that point, I will lay
Hard siege unto my mother, tho' I know
A siren's tongue could not bewitch her so.

[Enter Gratiana.]

[*Aside*] Mass, fitly here she comes; thanks, my disguise.--
Madam, good afternoon.

[GRATIANA]
Y'are welcome, sir.

VINDICI
The next of Italy commends him to you,
Our mighty expectation, the duke's son.

[GRATIANA]
I think myself much honour'd that he pleases
To rank me in his thoughts.

VINDICI
So may you, lady:
One that is like to be our sudden duke;
The crown gapes for him every tide, and then
Commander o'er us all. Do but think on him;
How bless'd were they now that could pleasure him
E'en with anything almost.

[GRATIANA]
Ay, save their honour.

VINDICI
Tut, one would let a little of that go too
And ne'er be seen in't: ne'er be seen [in't], mark you;
I'd wink and let it go.

[GRATIANA]
Marry, but I would not.

VINDICI
Marry, but I would I hope; I know you would too,
If you'd that blood now which you gave your daughter.
To her indeed 'tis this wheel comes about:
That man that must be all this, perhaps ere morning,
For his white father does but mould away,
Has long desir'd your daughter.

[GRATIANA]
Desir'd?

VINDICI
Nay, but hear me:
He desires now that will command hereafter.
Therefore be wise; I speak as more a friend
To you than him. Madam, I know y'are poor
And 'lack the day, there are too many poor ladies already:
Why should you vex the number? 'Tis despis'd.
Live wealthy, rightly understand the world,
And chide away that foolish country girl
Keeps company with your daughter, chastity.

[GRATIANA]
Oh, fie, fie,
The riches of the world cannot hire
A mother to such a most unnatural task!

VINDICI
No, but a thousand angels can:
Men have no power; angels must work you to't.
The world descends into such base-born evils
That forty angels can make fourscore devils.
There will be fools still, I perceive, still [fools].
Would I be poor, dejected, scorn'd of greatness,
Swept from the palace, and see other daughters
Spring with the dew a' th' court, having mine own
So much desir'd and lov'd by the duke's son?
No, I would raise my state upon her breast
And call her eyes my tenants; I would count
My yearly maintenance upon her cheeks,
Take coach upon her lip, and all her parts

Should keep men after men, and I would ride
In pleasure upon pleasure.
You took great pains for her, once when it was;
Let her requite it now, tho' it be but some:
You brought her forth; she may well bring you home.

[GRATIANA]
Oh, heavens! This overcomes me.

VINDICI
[*Aside*] Not, I hope, already?

[GRATIANA]
It is too strong for me; men know that know us:
We are so weak their words can overthrow us.
He touch'd me nearly, made my virtues bate
When his tongue struck upon my poor estate.

VINDICI
[*Aside*] I e'en quake to proceed; my spirit turns edge.
I fear me she's unmother'd, yet I'll venture:
"That woman is all male whom none can enter."--
What think you now, lady? Speak, are you wiser?
What said advancement to you? Thus it said:
The daughter's fall lifts up the mother's head.
Did it not, madam? But I'll swear it does
In many places; tut, this age fears no man:
"'Tis no shame to be bad, because 'tis common."

[GRATIANA]
Ay, that's the comfort on't.

VINDICI
[*Aside*] The comfort on't!--
[*Giving her gold*] I keep the best for last: can these persuade you
To forget heaven and--

[GRATIANA]
Ay, these are they--

VINDICI
[*Aside*] Oh!

[GRATIANA]
That enchant our sex; these are the means
That govern our affections. That woman
Will not be troubled with the mother long
That sees the comfortable shine of you;
I blush to think what for your sakes I'll do!

VINDICI
[*Aside*] Oh, suff'ring heaven, with thy invisible finger
E'en at this instant turn the precious side
Of both mine eye-balls inward, not to see myself!

[GRATIANA]
Look you, sir.

VINDICI
Holla.

[GRATIANA]
[*Giving him gold*] Let this thank your pains.

VINDICI
Oh, you're a kind [madam].

[GRATIANA]
I'll see how I can move.

VINDICI
Your words will sting.

[GRATIANA]
If she be still chaste I'll ne'er call her mine.

VINDICI
[*Aside*] Spoke truer than you meant it.

Enter Castiza.

[GRATIANA]
Daughter Castiza.

CASTIZA
Madam.

VINDICI
Oh, she's yonder.
Meet her.
[*Aside*] Troops of celestial soldiers guard her heart;
Yon dam has devils enough to take her part.

CASTIZA
Madam, what makes yon evil-offic'd man
In presence of you?

[GRATIANA]
Why?

CASTIZA
He lately brought
Immodest writing sent from the duke's son
To tempt me to dishonourable act.

[GRATIANA]
Dishonourable act? Good honourable fool,
That wouldst be honest 'cause thou wouldst be so,
Producing no one reason but thy will.
And 't 'as a good report, prettily commended,
But pray by whom? Mean people, ignorant people;
The better sort I'm sure cannot abide it.
And by what rule should we square out our lives
But by our betters actions? Oh, if thou knew'st
What 'twere to lose it, thou would never keep it!
But there's a cold curse laid upon all maids:
Whilst other[s] clip the sun, they clasp the shades!
Virginity is paradise, lock'd up.
You cannot come by yourselves without fee,
And 'twas decreed that man should keep the key!
Deny advancement, treasure, the duke's son!

CASTIZA
I cry you mercy. Lady, I mistook you.
Pray did you see my mother? Which way went you?
Pray God I have not lost her.

VINDICI
[*Aside*] Prettily put by.

[GRATIANA]
Are you as proud to me as coy to him?
Do you not know me now?

CASTIZA
Why, are you she?
The world's so chang'd, one shape into another:
It is a wise child now that knows her mother.

VINDICI
[*Aside*] Most right, i'faith.

[GRATIANA]
I owe your cheek my hand
For that presumption now, but I'll forget it.
Come, you shall leave those childish 'haviours
And understand your time; fortunes flow to you.
What, will you be a girl?
If all fear'd drowning that spy waves ashore,
Gold would grow rich and all the merchants poor.

CASTIZA
It is a pretty saying of a wicked one, but methinks now
It does not show so well out of your mouth,
Better in his.

VINDICI
[*Aside*] Faith, bad enough in both,
Were I in earnest, as I'll seem no less.--
I wonder, lady, your own mother's words
Cannot be taken, nor stand in full force.
'Tis honesty you urge. What's honesty?
'Tis but heavens beggar,
And what woman is so foolish to keep honesty,
And be not able to keep herself? No,
Times are grown wiser and will keep less charge:
A maid that has small portion now intends
To break up house and live upon her friends.
How bless'd are you; you have happiness alone:
Others must fall to thousands, you to one,
Sufficient in himself to make your forehead
Dazzle the world with jewels, and petitionary people
Start at your presence.

[GRATIANA]
Oh, if I were young,
I should be ravish'd!

CASTIZA
Ay, to lose your honour.

VINDICI
'Slid, how can you lose your honour
To deal with my lord's grace?
He'll add more honour to it by his title;
Your mother will tell you how.

[GRATIANA]
That I will.

VINDICI
Oh, think upon the pleasure of the palace:
Secured ease and state, the stirring meats,
Ready to move out of the dishes,
That e'en now quicken when they're eaten,
Banquets abroad by torch-light, musics, sports,
Bare-headed vassals that had ne'er the fortune
To keep on their own hats but let horns [wear] 'em,
Nine coaches waiting. Hurry, hurry, hurry!

CASTIZA
Ay, to the devil.

VINDICI
[*Aside*] Ay, to the devil!--To th' duke, by my faith.

[GRATIANA]
Ay, to the duke: daughter, you'd scorn to think
A' th' devil and you were there once.

VINDICI
True, for most
There are as proud as he for his heart, i'faith.
Who'd sit at home in a neglected room,
Dealing her short-liv'd beauty to the pictures
That are as useless as old men, when those
Poorer in face and fortune than herself
Walk with a hundred acres on their backs,

Fair meadows cut into green foreparts? Oh,
It was the greatest blessing ever happened to women
When farmers' sons agreed, and met again,
To wash their hands and come up gentlemen;
The commonwealth has flourish'd ever since.
Lands that were [mete] by the rod, that labours spar'd:
Tailors ride down, and measure 'em by the yard.
Fair trees, those comely foretops of the field,
Are cut to maintain head-tires, much untold.
All thrives but chastity; she lies a-cold.
Nay, shall I come nearer to you? Mark but this:
Why are there so few honest women but
Because 'tis the poorer profession?
That's accounted best that's best followed:
Least in trade, least in fashion,
And that's not honesty. Believe it, and do
But note the [low] and dejected price of it:
"Lose but a pearl, we search and cannot brook it,
But that once gone, who is so mad to look it?"

[GRATIANA]
Troth, he says true.

CASTIZA
False! I defy you both!
I have endur'd you with an ear of fire;
Your tongues have struck hot irons on my face!
Mother, come from that poisonous woman there.

[GRATIANA]
Where?

CASTIZA
Do you not see her? She's too inward then.
Slave, perish in thy office! You heavens, please
Henceforth to make the mother a disease,
Which first begins with me, yet I've outgone you.

Exit.

VINDICI
[*Aside*] Oh angels, clap your wings upon the skies,
And give this virgin crystal plaudities!

[GRATIANA]
Peevish, coy, foolish! But return this answer:
My lord shall be most welcome when his pleasure
Conducts him this way. I will sway mine own;
Women with women can work best alone.

VINDICI
Indeed, I'll tell him so.

Exit.

Oh, more uncivil, more unnatural,
Than those base-titled creatures that look downward!
Why does not heaven [turn] black, or with a frown
Undo the world? Why does not earth start up
And strike the sins that tread upon't? Oh,
Wert not gold and women, there would be no damnation;
Hell would look like a lord's great kitchen without fire in't!
But 'twas decreed before the world began
That they should be the hooks to catch at man.

Exit.

[II.ii. The palace]

Enter Lussurioso with Hippolito, Vindici's brother.

LUSSURIOSO
I much applaud thy judgment; thou art well-read in a fellow,
And 'tis the deepest art to study man.
I know this, which I never learnt in schools:
The world's divided into knaves and fools.

HIPPOLITO
[*Aside*] Knave in your face, my lord, behind your back.

LUSSURIOSO
And I much thank thee that thou hast preferr'd
A fellow of discourse, well-mingled,
And whose brain time hath season'd.

HIPPOLITO
True, my lord.
[*Aside*] We shall find season once I hope. Oh, villain,
To make such an unnatural slave of me! But--

[Enter Vindici, disguised as Piato.]

LUSSURIOSO
Mass, here he comes.

HIPPOLITO
[Aside] And now shall I have free leave to depart.

LUSSURIOSO
Your absence; leave us.

HIPPOLITO
[Aside] Are not my thoughts true?
I must remove; but brother, you may stay:
Heart, we are both made bawds a new-found way!

Exit.

LUSSURIOSO
Now we're an even number; a third man's dangerous,
Especially her brother. Say, be free:
Have I a pleasure toward?

VINDICI
Oh, my lord!

LUSSURIOSO
Ravish me in thine answer. Art thou rare?
Hast thou beguil'd her of salvation,
And rubb'd hell o'er with honey? Is she a woman?

VINDICI
In all but in desire.

LUSSURIOSO
Then she's in nothing;
I bate in courage now.

VINDICI
The words I brought,
Might well have made indifferent-honest naught.
A right good woman in these days is chang'd
Into white money with less labour far:
Many a maid has turn'd to Mahomet
With easier working. I durst undertake

Upon the pawn and forfeit of my life
With half those words to flat a Puritan's wife,
But she is close and good. Yet 'tis a doubt
By this time: oh, the mother, the mother!

LUSSURIOSO
I never thought their sex had been a wonder
Until this minute. What fruit from the mother?

VINDICI
[*Aside*] Now must I blister my soul, be forsworn,
Or shame the woman that receiv'd me first.
I will be true; thou liv'st not to proclaim:
Spoke to a dying man, shame has no shame.--
My lord.

LUSSURIOSO
Who's that?

VINDICI
Here's none but I, my lord.

LUSSURIOSO
What would thy haste utter?

VINDICI
Comfort.

LUSSURIOSO
Welcome.

VINDICI
The maid being dull, having no mind to travel
Into unknown lands, what did me straight
But set spurs to the mother; golden spurs
Will put her to a false gallop in a trice.

LUSSURIOSO
Is't possible that in this
The mother should be damn'd before the daughter?

VINDICI
Oh, that's good manners, my lord; the mother
For her age must go foremost, you know.

LUSSURIOSO
Thou'st spoke that true! But where comes in this comfort?

VINDICI
In a fine place, my lord. The unnatural mother
Did with her tongue so hard beset her honour
That the poor fool was struck to silent wonder,
Yet still the maid like an unlighted taper
Was cold and chaste, save that her mothers breath
Did blow fire on her [cheeks]; the girl departed,
But the good, ancient madam half-mad threw me
These promising words, which I took deeply note of:
"My lord shall be most welcome"--

LUSSURIOSO
Faith, I thank her.

VINDICI
"When his pleasure conducts him this way"--

LUSSURIOSO
That shall be soon, i'faith.

VINDICI
"I will sway mine own"--

LUSSURIOSO
She does the wiser; I commend her for't.

VINDICI
"Women with women can work best alone."

LUSSURIOSO
By this light, and so they can. Give 'em their due;
Men are not comparable to 'em.

VINDICI
No,
That's true, for you shall have one woman knit
More in a hour than any man can ravel
Again in seven and twenty year.

LUSSURIOSO
Now my
Desires are happy, I'll make 'em freemen now.

43

Thou art a precious fellow; faith, I love thee.
Be wise and make it thy revenue: beg, leg!
What office couldst thou be ambitious for?

VINDICI
Office, my lord? Marry, if I might have my wish
I would have one that was never begg'd yet.

LUSSURIOSO
Nay, then thou canst have none.

VINDICI
Yes, my lord,
I could pick out another office yet,
Nay, and keep a horse and drab upon't.

LUSSURIOSO
Prithee, good bluntness, tell me.

VINDICI
Why I would desire but this,
My lord: to have all the fees behind the arras,
And all the farthingales that fall plump
About twelve a' clock at night upon the rushes.

LUSSURIOSO
Thou'rt a mad, apprehensive knave.
Dost think to make any great purchase of that?

VINDICI
Oh, 'tis an unknown thing,
My lord; I wonder 't 'as been miss'd so long.

LUSSURIOSO
Well, this night I'll visit her, and 'tis till then
A year in my desires. Farewell, attend,
Trust me with thy preferment.

VINDICI
My lov'd lord!

Exit.

Oh, shall I kill him a' th' wrong side now? No.
Sword, thou wast never a back-biter yet.

I'll pierce him to his face; he shall die looking upon me.
Thy veins are swell'd with lust; this shall unfill 'em:
Great men were gods if beggars could not kill 'em.
Forgive me, heaven, to call my mother wicked;
Oh, lessen not my days upon the earth!
I cannot honour her; by this I fear me
Her tongue has turn'd my sister into use.
I was a villain not to be forsworn
To this our lecherous hope, the duke's son,
For lawyers, merchants, some divines and all
Count beneficial perjury a sin small.
It shall go hard yet, but I'll guard her honour
And keep the ports sure.

Enter Hippolito.

HIPPOLITO
Brother, how goes the world? I would know news of you,
But I have news to tell you.

VINDICI
What, in the name of knavery?

HIPPOLITO
Knavery? Faith,
This vicious old duke's worthily abus'd:
The pen of his bastard writes him cuckold!

VINDICI
His bastard?

HIPPOLITO
Pray, believe it: he and the duchess
By night meet in their linen; they have been seen
By stair-foot panders!

VINDICI
Oh, sin foul and deep,
Great faults are wink'd at when the duke's asleep!

[Enter Spurio and his two Servants, one whispering to him.]

See, see, here comes the Spurio.

HIPPOLITO
Monstrous luxur!

VINDICI
Unbrac'd, two of his valiant bawds with him.
Oh, there's a wicked whisper; hell is in his ear!
Stay, let's observe his passage.

[They retire.]

SPURIO
Oh, but are you sure on't?

[FIRST] SERVANT
My lord, most sure on't, for 'twas spoke by one
That is most inward with the duke's son's lust,
That he intends within this hour to steal
Unto Hippolito's sister, whose chaste life
The mother has corrupted for his use.

SPURIO
Sweet world, sweet occasion! Faith, then, brother
I'll disinherit you in as short time,
As I was when I was begot in haste:
I'll damn you at your pleasure: precious deed
After your lust; oh, 'twill be fine to bleed!
Come, let our passing out be soft and wary.

Exeunt [Spurio and Servants].

VINDICI
Mark, there, there, that step! Now to the duchess:
This their second meeting writes the duke cuckold
With new additions, his horns newly reviv'd.
Night, thou that lookst like funeral heralds' fees
Torn down betimes i' th' morning, thou hang'st fitly
To grace those sins that have no grace at all.
Now 'tis full sea a-bed over the world;
There's juggling of all sides. Some that were maids
E'en at sunset are now perhaps i' th' toll-book:
This woman in immodest, thin apparel
Lets in her friend by water; here a dame
Cunning nails leather hinges to a door,
To avoid proclamation.

Now cuckolds are a-coining, apace, apace, apace, apace;
And careful sisters spin that thread i' th' night
That does maintain them and their bawds i' th' day!

HIPPOLITO
You flow well, brother.

VINDICI
Puh, I'm shallow yet,
Too sparing and too modest. Shall I tell thee?
If every trick were told that's dealt by night,
There are few here that would not blush outright.

HIPPOLITO
I am of that belief too.

Enter Lussurioso.

VINDICI
[*Aside to Hippolito*] Who's this comes?
The duke's son up so late! Brother, fall back,
And you shall learn some mischief.--My good lord.

LUSSURIOSO
Piato! Why, the man I wish'd for. Come,
I do embrace this season for the fittest
To taste of that young lady.

VINDICI
[*Aside*] Heart and hell!

HIPPOLITO
[*Aside*] Damn'd villain!

VINDICI
[*Aside*] I ha' no way now to cross it but to kill him.

LUSSURIOSO
Come, only thou and I.

VINDICI
My lord, my lord.

LUSSURIOSO
Why dost thou start us?

VINDICI
I'd almost forgot: the bastard!

LUSSURIOSO
What of him?

VINDICI
This night, this hour, this minute, now!

LUSSURIOSO
What! What!

VINDICI
Shadows the duchess--

LUSSURIOSO
Horrible word.

VINDICI
And like strong poison eats
Into the duke your father's forehead.

LUSSURIOSO
Oh!

VINDICI
He makes horn royal.

LUSSURIOSO
Most ignoble slave!

VINDICI
This is the fruit of two beds.

LUSSURIOSO
I am mad!

VINDICI
That passage he trod warily.

LUSSURIOSO
He did!

VINDICI
And hush'd his villains every step he took.

LUSSURIOSO
His villains! I'll confound them!

VINDICI
Take 'em finely, finely now.

LUSSURIOSO
The duchess' chamber-door shall not control me.

[Exeunt Lussurioso and Vindici.]

HIPPOLITO
Good, happy, swift; there's gunpowder i' th' court,
Wildfire at midnight in this heedless fury.
He may show violence to cross himself;
I'll follow the event.

Exit.

[II.iii. The Duke's bedchamber]

[The Duke and Duchess are discovered in bed. Lussurioso and Vindici] enter again [with Hippolito following].

LUSSURIOSO
Where is that villain?

VINDICI
Softly, my lord, and you may take 'em twisted.

LUSSURIOSO
I care not how!

VINDICI
Oh, 'twill be glorious
To kill 'em doubled, when they're heap'd! Be soft, my lord.

LUSSURIOSO
Away! My [spleen] is not so lazy; thus and thus
I'll shake their eyelids ope, and with my sword
Shut 'em again forever.

[He draws his sword and approaches the bed.]

Villain, strumpet!

DUKE
You upper guard defend us!

DUCHESS
Treason, treason!

DUKE
Oh, take me not in sleep; I have great sins: I must have days,
Nay, months, dear son, with penitential heaves
To lift 'em out and not to die unclear!
Oh, thou wilt kill me both in heaven and here!

LUSSURIOSO
I am amaz'd to death.

DUKE
Nay, villain traitor,
Worse than the foulest epithet, now I'll gripe thee
E'en with the nerves of wrath, and throw thy head
Amongst the lawyer's! Guard!

Enter Nobles and sons [Ambitioso and Supervacuo, with guards].

FIRST NOBLE
How comes the quiet of your grace disturb'd?

DUKE
This boy that should be myself after me
Would be myself before me, and in heat
Of that ambition bloodily rush'd in
Intending to depose me in my bed.

SECOND NOBLE
Duty and natural loyalty forfend!

DUCHESS
He call'd his father villain and me strumpet,
A word that I abhor to 'file my lips with.

AMBITIOSO
That was not so well done, brother.

LUSSURIOSO
I am abus'd.
I know there's no excuse can do me good.

VINDICI
[*Aside to Hippolito*] 'Tis now good policy to be from sight;
His vicious purpose to our sister's honour
Is cross'd beyond our thought.

HIPPOLITO
[*Aside to Vindici*] You little dreamt his father slept here.

VINDICI
[*Aside to Hippolito*] Oh, 'twas far beyond me.
But since it fell so-- Without frightful word,
Would he had kill'd him, 'twould have eas'd our swords.

DUKE
Be comforted, our duchess: he shall die.

[The Duchess exits as the guards seize Lussurioso. Vindici and Hippolito] dissemble a flight.

LUSSURIOSO
Where's this slave-pander now? Out of mine eye,
Guilty of this abuse.

Enter Spurio with his villains [to one side].

SPURIO
Y'are villains, fablers;
You have knaves' chins and harlots' tongues: you lie,
And I will damn you with one meal a day.

FIRST SERVANT
Oh, good my lord!

SPURIO
'Sblood, you shall never sup.

SECOND SERVANT
Oh, I beseech you, sir!

SPURIO
To let my sword catch cold so long and miss him!

FIRST SERVANT
Troth, my lord, 'twas his intent to meet there.

SPURIO
Heart, he's yonder!
Ha! What news here? Is the day out a' th' socket
That it is noon at midnight? The court up?
How comes the guard so saucy with his elbows?

LUSSURIOSO
The bastard here?
Nay, then the truth of my intent shall out.
My lord and father, hear me.

DUKE
Bear him hence.

LUSSURIOSO
I can with loyalty excuse.

DUKE
Excuse? To prison with the villain;
Death shall not long lag after him.

SPURIO
[*Aside*] Good, i'faith, then 'tis not much amiss.

LUSSURIOSO
[*To Ambitioso and Supervacuo aside*] Brothers, my best release lies on your
tongues;
I pray persuade for me.

AMBITIOSO
It is our duties: make yourself sure of us.

SUPERVACUO
We'll sweat in pleading.

LUSSURIOSO
And I may live to thank you.

Exeunt [Lussurioso and guards].

AMBITIOSO
[*Aside*] No, thy death shall thank me better.

SPURIO
He's gone: I'll after him

And know his trespass, seem to bear a part
In all his ills, but with a puritan heart.

Exit [with Servants].

AMBITIOSO
[*Aside to Supervacuo*] Now, brother, let our hate and love be woven
So subtly together, that in speaking one word for his life,
We may make three for his death:
The craftiest pleader gets most gold for breath.

SUPERVACUO
[*Aside to Ambitioso*] Set on; I'll not be far behind you, brother.

DUKE
Is't possible a son
Should be disobedient as far as the sword?
It is the highest; he can go no farther.

AMBITIOSO
My gracious lord, take pity--

DUKE
Pity, boys?

AMBITIOSO
Nay, we'd be loath to move your grace too much;
We know the trespass is unpardonable,
Black, wicked, and unnatural.

SUPERVACUO
In a son, oh, monstrous!

AMBITIOSO
Yet, my lord,
A duke's soft hand strokes the rough head of law
And makes it lie smooth.

DUKE
But my hand shall ne'er do't.

AMBITIOSO
That as you please, my lord.

SUPERVACUO
We must needs confess
Some father would have enter'd into hate,
So deadly pointed, that before his eyes
He would ha' seen the execution sound
Without corrupted favour.

AMBITIOSO
But, my lord,
Your grace may live the wonder of all times
In pard'ning that offence which never yet
Had face to beg a pardon.

DUKE
Honey? How's this?

AMBITIOSO
Forgive him, good my lord: he's your own son,
And I must needs say 'twas the vildlier done.

SUPERVACUO
He's the next heir, yet this true reason gathers:
None can possess that dispossess their fathers.
Be merciful--

DUKE
[*Aside*] Here's no stepmother's wit:
I'll try 'em both upon their love and hate.

AMBITIOSO
Be merciful, although--

DUKE
You have prevail'd:
My wrath like flaming wax hath spent itself.
I know 'twas but some peevish moon in him:
Go, let him be releas'd.

SUPERVACUO
[*Aside to Ambitioso*] 'Sfoot, how now, brother?

AMBITIOSO
Your grace doth please to speak beside your spleen;
I would it were so happy.

DUKE
Why, go, release him.

SUPERVACUO
Oh, my good lord, I know the fault's too weighty
And full of general loathing, too inhuman,
Rather by all men's voices worthy death.

DUKE
'Tis true too.
Here then, receive this signet; doom shall pass:
Direct it to the judges; he shall die
Ere many days. Make haste.

AMBITIOSO
All speed that may be.
We could have wish'd his burthen not so sore;
We knew your grace did but delay before.

Exeunt [Ambitioso and Supervacuo].

DUKE
Here's envy with a poor, thin cover o'er 't,
Like scarlet hid in lawn, easily spied through.
This their ambition by the mother's side
Is dangerous, and for safety must be purg'd;
I will prevent their envies. Sure it was
But some mistaken fury in our son,
Which these aspiring boys would climb upon:
He shall be releas'd suddenly.

Enter Nobles. [They kneel.]

FIRST NOBLE
Good morning to your grace.

DUKE
Welcome, my lords.

SECOND NOBLE
Our knees shall take away the office of our feet forever,
Unless your grace bestow a father's eye
Upon the clouded fortunes of your son,

And in compassionate virtue grant him that
Which makes e'en mean men happy: liberty.

DUKE
[*Aside*] How seriously their loves and honours woo
For that which I am about to pray them do!--
Rise, my lords, your knees sign his release:
We freely pardon him.

FIRST NOBLE
We owe your grace much thanks, and he much duty.

Exeunt [Nobles].

DUKE
It well becomes that judge to nod at crimes
That does commit greater himself and lives.
I may forgive a disobedient error
That expect pardon for adultery,
And in my old days am a youth in lust:
Many a beauty have I turn'd to poison
In the denial, covetous of all.
Age hot is like a monster to be seen:
My hairs are white, and yet my sins are green.

[Exit.]

III.[i. The palace]

Enter Ambitioso and Supervacuo.

SUPERVACUO
Brother, let my opinion sway you once,
I speak it for the best, to have him die
Surest and soonest; if the signet come
Unto the judges' hands, why, then his doom
Will be deferr'd till sittings and court-days,
Juries and further. Faiths are bought and sold;
Oaths in these days are but the skin of gold.

AMBITIOSO
In troth, 'tis true too!

SUPERVACUO
Then let's set by the judges

And fall to the officers; 'tis but mistaking
The duke our father's meaning, and where he nam'd
"Ere many days," 'tis but forgetting that
And have him die i' th' morning.

AMBITIOSO
Excellent;
Then am I heir, duke in a minute.

SUPERVACUO
[*Aside*] Nay,
And he were once puff'd out, here is a pin
Should quickly prick your bladder.

AMBITIOSO
[Bless'd] occasion!
He being pack'd, we'll have some trick and wile
To wind our younger brother out of prison
That lies in for the rape; the lady's dead,
And people's thoughts will soon be buried.

SUPERVACUO
We may with safety do't, and live and feed;
The duchess' sons are too proud to bleed.

AMBITIOSO
We are, i'faith, to say true. Come, let's not linger.
I'll to the officers; go you before
And set an edge upon the executioner.

SUPERVACUO
Let me alone to grind him.

AMBITIOSO
Meet; farewell.

Exit [Supervacuo].

I am next now; I rise just in that place
Where thou'rt cut off: upon thy neck, kind brother.
The falling of one head lifts up another.

Exit.

[III.ii. Outside the prison]

Enter with the Nobles, Lussurioso from prison.

LUSSURIOSO
My lords, I am so much indebted to your loves
For this, oh, this delivery!

FIRST NOBLE
But our duties,
My lord, unto the hopes that grow in you.

LUSSURIOSO
If e'er I live to be myself, I'll thank you.
Oh liberty, thou sweet and heavenly dame!
But hell for prison is too mild a name.

Exeunt.

[III.iii. The prison]

Enter Ambitioso and Supervacuo, with Officers.

AMBITIOSO
Officers, here's the duke's signet, your firm warrant,
Brings the command of present death along with it
Unto our brother, the duke's son; we are sorry
That we are so unnaturally employ'd
In such an unkind office, fitter far
For enemies than brothers.

SUPERVACUO
But you know,
The duke's command must be obey'd.

FIRST OFFICER
It must and shall my lord; this morning then.
So suddenly?

AMBITIOSO
Ay, alas, poor good soul,
He must breakfast betimes; the executioner
Stands ready to put forth his cowardly valour.

SECOND OFFICER
Already?

SUPERVACUO
Already, i'faith. Oh, sir, destruction hies,
And that is least impudent soonest dies.

FIRST OFFICER
Troth, you say true, my lord. We take our leaves;
Our office shall be sound: we'll not delay
The third part of a minute.

AMBITIOSO
Therein you show
Yourselves good men and upright officers.
Pray let him die as private as he may;
Do him that favour, for the gaping people
Will but trouble him at his prayers
And make him curse and swear, and so die black.
Will you be so far kind?

FIRST OFFICER
It shall be done, my lord.

AMBITIOSO
Why, we do thank you; if we live to be,
You shall have a better office.

SECOND OFFICER
Your good lordship.

SUPERVACUO
Commend us to the scaffold in our tears.

FIRST OFFICER
We'll weep and do your commendations.

Exeunt [Officers].

AMBITIOSO
Fine fools in office!

SUPERVACUO
Things fall out so fit.

AMBITIOSO
So happily! Come, brother, ere next clock
His head will be made serve a bigger block.

Exeunt.

[III.iv. Junior brother's cell in the prison]

Enter in prison Junior brother.

JUNIOR
Keeper.

[Enter the Keeper.]

KEEPER
My lord.

JUNIOR
No news lately from our brothers?
Are they unmindful of us?

KEEPER
My lord, a messenger came newly in
And brought this from 'em.

[He hands him a letter.]

JUNIOR
Nothing but paper comforts?
I look'd for my delivery before this
Had they been worth their oaths. Prithee be from us.

[Exit the Keeper.]

Now what say you, forsooth? Speak out, I pray.

[Opens and reads the] letter.

"Brother be of good cheer."
'Slud, it begins like a whore with good cheer!
"Thou shalt not be long a prisoner."
Not five and thirty year like a bankrout, I think so.
"We have thought upon a device to get thee out by a trick."
By a trick! Pox a' your trick and it be so long a-playing!
"And so rest comforted, be merry and expect it suddenly."
Be merry, hang merry, draw and quarter merry, I'll be mad!
Is't not strange that a man should lie in a whole month for a woman? Well,

we shall see how sudden our brothers will be in their promise. I must expect still a trick! I shall not be long a prisoner!

[Enter the Keeper with four Officers.]

How now, what news?

KEEPER
Bad news, my lord; I am discharg'd of you.

JUNIOR
Slave, call'st thou that bad news? I thank you, brothers!

KEEPER
My lord, 'twill prove so; here come the officers
Into whose hands I must commit you.

JUNIOR
Ha, officers? What, why?

FIRST OFFICER
You must pardon us, my lord;
Our office must be sound: here is our warrant,
The signet from the duke; you must straight suffer.

JUNIOR
Suffer? I'll suffer you to be gone, I'll suffer you
To come no more! What would you have me suffer?

SECOND OFFICER
My lord, those words were better chang'd to prayers;
The time's but brief with you: prepare to die.

JUNIOR
Sure 'tis not so.

THIRD OFFICER
It is too true, my lord.

JUNIOR
I tell you 'tis not, for the duke my father
Deferr'd me till next sitting, and I look
E'en every minute, threescore times an hour,
For a release, a trick wrought by my brothers.

FIRST OFFICER
A trick, my lord? If you expect such comfort,
Your hopes as fruitless as a barren woman:
Your brothers were the unhappy messengers
That brought this powerful token for your death.

JUNIOR
My brothers? No, no!

SECOND OFFICER
'Tis most true, my lord.

JUNIOR
My brothers to bring a warrant for my death?
How strange this shows!

THIRD OFFICER
There's no delaying time.

JUNIOR
Desire 'em hither, call 'em up, my brothers!
They shall deny it to your faces.

FIRST OFFICER
My lord,
They're far enough by this, at least at court,
And this most strict command they left behind 'em,
When grief swum in their eyes: they show'd like brothers,
Brimful of heavy sorrow; but the duke
Must have his pleasure.

JUNIOR
His pleasure?

FIRST OFFICER
These were their last words which my memory bears:
"Commend us to the scaffold in our tears."

JUNIOR
Pox dry their tears! What should I do with tears?
I hate 'em worse than any citizen's son
Can hate salt water. Here came a letter now,
New-bleeding from their pens, scarce stinted yet;
Would I'd been torn in pieces when I tore it.

Look, you officious whoresons, words of comfort:
"Not long a prisoner."

FIRST OFFICER
It says true in that, sir, for you must suffer presently.

JUNIOR
A villainous duns upon the letter! Knavish exposition! Look you then here,
sir: "we'll get thee out by a trick," says he.

SECOND OFFICER
That may hold too, sir, for you know a trick is commonly four cards, which
was meant by us four officers.

JUNIOR
Worse and worse dealing!

FIRST OFFICER
The hour beckons us.
The heads-man waits; lift up your eyes to heaven.

JUNIOR
I thank you, faith; good, pretty, wholesome counsel.
I should look up to heaven, as you said,
Whilst he behind me cozens me of my head;
Ay, that's the trick.

THIRD OFFICER
You delay too long, my lord.

JUNIOR
Stay, good authority's bastards, since I must
Through brothers' perjury die, oh, let me venom
Their souls with curses!

FIRST OFFICER
Come, 'tis no time to curse.

JUNIOR
Must I bleed then without respect of sign? Well,
My fault was sweet sport, which the world approves;
I die for that which every woman loves.

Exeunt.

[III.v. A lodge]

Enter Vindici with Hippolito his brother.

VINDICI
Oh, sweet, delectable, rare, happy, ravishing!

HIPPOLITO
Why, what's the matter, brother?

VINDICI
Oh, 'tis able
To make a man spring up and knock his forehead
Against yon silver ceiling!

HIPPOLITO
Prithee tell me.
Why, may not I partake with you? You vow'd once
To give me share to every tragic thought.

VINDICI
By th' mass, I think I did too.
Then I'll divide it to thee: the old duke
Thinking my outward shape and inward heart
Are cut out of one piece--for he that prates his secrets,
His heart stands a' th' outside--hires me by price
To greet him with a lady
In some fit place veil'd from the eyes a' th' court,
Some dark'ned, blushless angle, that is guilty
Of his forefathers' lusts and great-folks' riots,
To which I easily, to maintain my shape,
Consented, and did wish his impudent grace
To meet her here in this unsunned lodge,
Wherein 'tis night at noon, and here the rather,
Because unto the torturing of his soul
The bastard and the duchess have appointed
Their meeting too in this luxurious circle,
Which most afflicting sight will kill his eyes
Before we kill the rest of him.

HIPPOLITO
'Twill, i'faith, most dreadfully digested.
I see not how you could have miss'd me, brother.

VINDICI
True, but the violence of my joy forgot it.

HIPPOLITO
Ay, but where's that lady now?

VINDICI
Oh, at that word
I'm lost again; you cannot find me yet:
I'm in a throng of happy apprehensions!
He's suited for a lady; I have took care
For a delicious lip, a sparkling eye:
You shall be witness brother.
Be ready; stand with your hat off.

Exit.

HIPPOLITO
Troth, I wonder what lady it should be?
Yet 'tis no wonder, now I think again,
To have a lady stoop to a duke that stoops unto his men.
'Tis common to be common through the world:
And there's more private common shadowing vices
Than those who are known both by their names and prices.
[*Taking off his hat*] 'Tis part of my allegiance to stand bare
To the duke's concubine, and here she comes.

Enter [Vindici] with the skull of his love dress'd up in tires.

VINDICI
Madam, his grace will not be absent long.
Secret? Ne'er doubt us, madam; 'twill be worth
Three velvet gowns to your ladyship. Known?
Few ladies respect that. Disgrace? A poor, thin shell;
'Tis the best grace you have to do it well.
I'll save your hand that labour; I'll unmask you.

[Draws back the tires.]

HIPPOLITO
Why, brother, brother!

VINDICI
Art thou beguil'd now? Tut, a lady can

At such, all hid, beguile a wiser man.
Have I not fitted the old surfeiter
With a quaint piece of beauty? Age and bare bone
Are e'er allied in action: here's an eye
Able to tempt a great man to serve God,
A pretty, hanging lip that has forgot now to dissemble;
Methinks this mouth should make a swearer tremble,
A drunkard clasp his teeth and not undo 'em
To suffer wet damnation to run through 'em.
Here's a cheek keeps her colour, let the wind go whistle:
Spout rain, we fear thee not; be hot or cold
Alls one with us. And is not he absurd
Whose fortunes are upon their faces set,
That fear no other God but wind and wet?

HIPPOLITO
Brother, y'ave spoke that right.
Is this the form that living shone so bright?

VINDICI
The very same;
And now methinks I [could] e'en chide myself
For doting on her beauty, tho' her death
Shall be reveng'd after no common action.
Does the silkworm expend her yellow labours
For thee? For thee does she undo herself?
Are lordships sold to maintain ladyships
For the poor benefit of a bewitching minute?
Why does yon fellow falsify highways
And put his life between the judge's lips
To refine such a thing, keeps horse and men
To beat their valours for her?
Surely we're all mad people, and they
Whom we think are, are not; we mistake those:
'Tis we are mad in sense, they but in clothes.

HIPPOLITO
Faith, and in clothes too we; give us our due.

VINDICI
Does every proud and self-affecting dame
Camphor her face for this, and grieve her maker
In sinful baths of milk, when many an infant starves,
For her superfluous outside fall for this?

Who now bids twenty pound a-night, prepares
Music, perfumes, and sweetmeats? All are hush'd;
Thou mayst lie chaste now! It were fine, methinks,
To have thee seen at revels, forgetful feasts,
And unclean brothels; sure 'twould fright the sinner
And make him a good coward, put a reveller
Out of his antic amble,
And cloy an epicure with empty dishes.
Here might a scornful and ambitious woman
Look through and through herself; see, ladies, with false forms
You deceive men but cannot deceive worms.
Now to my tragic business. Look you, brother,
I have not fashion'd this only for show
And useless property; no, it shall bear a part
E'en in [its] own revenge.

[Applies poison to the skull's mouth.]

This very skull,
Whose mistress the duke poisoned, with this drug,
The mortal curse of the earth, shall be reveng'd
In the like strain, and kiss his lips to death.
As much as the dumb thing can, he shall feel:
What fails in poison, we'll supply in steel.

HIPPOLITO
Brother, I do applaud thy constant vengeance,
The quaintness of thy malice above thought.

VINDICI
So 'tis laid on. Now come and welcome, duke;
I have her for thee. I protest it, brother:
Methinks she makes almost as fair a sign
As some old gentlewoman in a periwig.
Hide thy face now for shame; thou hadst need have a mask now:
'Tis vain when beauty flows, but when it fleets,
This would become graves better than the streets.

HIPPOLITO
You have my voice in that. Hark, the duke's come!

VINDICI
Peace, let's observe what company he brings,
And how he does absent 'em, for you know

He'll wish all private: brother, fall you back a little
With the bony lady.

HIPPOLITO
That I will.

VINDICI
So, so: now nine years' vengeance crowd into a minute!

[Enter the Duke talking to his Gentlemen.]

DUKE
You shall have leave to leave us, with this charge:
Upon your lives, if we be miss'd by th' duchess
Or any of the nobles, to give out
We're privately rid forth.

VINDICI
[Aside] Oh, happiness!

DUKE
With some few honourable gentlemen, you may say;
You may name those that are away from court.

[FIRST] GENTLEMAN
Your will and pleasure shall be done, my lord.

[Exeunt the Gentlemen.]

VINDICI
[Aside] Privately rid forth!
He strives to make sure work on't.--Your good grace?

DUKE
Piato, well done. Hast brought her? What lady is't?

VINDICI
Faith, my lord, a country lady, a little bashful at first, as most of them are, but
after the first kiss, my lord, the worst is past with them. Your grace knows
now what you have to do; sh'as somewhat a grave look with her, but--

DUKE
I love that best: conduct her.

VINDICI
Have at all.

DUKE
In gravest looks the greatest faults seem less;
Give me that sin that's rob'd in holiness.

VINDICI
[*Aside to Hippolito*] Back with the torch; brother, raise the perfumes.

DUKE
How sweet can a duke [breathe]? Age has no fault;
Pleasure should meet in a perfumed mist.
Lady, sweetly encount'red. I came from court:
I must be bold with you--

[*Kisses the skull.*]

Oh, what's this? Oh!

VINDICI
Royal villain, white devil!

DUKE
Oh!

VINDICI
Brother,
Place the torch here, that his affrighted eyeballs
May start into those hollows. Duke, dost know
Yon dreadful vizard? View it well: 'tis the skull
Of Gloriana, whom thou poisoned'st last.

DUKE
Oh, 't 'as poisoned me!

VINDICI
Didst not know that till now?

DUKE
What are you two?

VINDICI
Villains all three! The very ragged bone
Has been sufficiently reveng'd!

DUKE
Oh, Hippolito? Call treason!

HIPPOLITO *stamping on him*
Yes, my good lord: treason, treason, treason!

DUKE
Then I'm betray'd!

VINDICI
Alas, poor lecher in the hands of knaves:
A slavish duke is baser than his slaves.

DUKE
My teeth are eaten out!

VINDICI
Hadst any left?

HIPPOLITO
I think but few.

VINDICI
Then those that did eat are eaten.

DUKE
Oh, my tongue!

VINDICI
Your tongue? 'Twill teach you to kiss closer,
Not like a [slobbering] Dutchman! You have eyes still:
Look, monster, what a lady hast thou made me,
My once betrothed wife!

DUKE
Is it thou, villain? Nay, then--

VINDICI
'Tis I, 'tis Vindici, 'tis I!

HIPPOLITO
And let this comfort thee: our lord and father
Fell sick upon the infection of thy frowns
And died in sadness; be that thy hope of life!

DUKE
Oh!

VINDICI
He had his tongue, yet grief made him die speechless.
Puh, 'tis but early yet; now I'll begin
To stick thy soul with ulcers, I will make
Thy spirit grievous sore: it shall not rest,
But like some pestilent man toss in thy breast. Mark me, duke,
Thou'rt a renowned, high, and mighty cuckold.

DUKE
Oh!

VINDICI
Thy bastard, thy bastard rides a-hunting in thy brow.

DUKE
Millions of deaths!

VINDICI
Nay, to afflict thee more,
Here in this lodge they meet for damned clips;
Those eyes shall see the incest of their lips.

DUKE
Is there a hell besides this, villains?

VINDICI
Villain?
Nay, heaven is just: scorns are the hires of scorns;
I ne'er knew yet adulterer without horns.

HIPPOLITO
Once ere they die 'tis quitted.

[Music within.]

VINDICI
Hark, the music!
Their banquet is prepar'd; they're coming.

DUKE
Oh, kill me not with that sight!

VINDICI
Thou shalt not lose that sight for all thy dukedom.

DUKE
Traitors, murderers!

VINDICI
What? Is not thy tongue eaten out yet?
Then we'll invent a silence. Brother, stifle the torch.

DUKE
Treason, murther!

VINDICI
Nay, faith, we'll have you hush'd now with thy dagger.
Nail down his tongue, and mine shall keep possession
About his heart: if he but gasp he dies;
We dread not death to quittance injuries. Brother,
If he but wink, not brooking the foul object,
Let our two other hands tear up his lids,
And make his eyes like comets shine through blood;
When the bad bleeds, then is the tragedy good.

HIPPOLITO
Whist, brother: music's at our ear, they come.

Enter [Spurio] the bastard meeting the Duchess. [They kiss.]

SPURIO
Had not that kiss a taste of sin, 'twere sweet.

DUCHESS
Why, there's no pleasure sweet but it is sinful.

SPURIO
True, such a bitter sweetness fate hath given;
Best side to us is the worst side to heaven.

DUCHESS
Push, come: 'tis the old duke thy doubtful father;
The thought of him rubs heaven in thy way,
But I protest by yonder waxen fire,
Forget him or I'll poison him.

SPURIO
Madam, you urge a thought which ne'er had life.
So deadly do I loathe him for my birth,
That if he took me hasp'd within his bed,
I would add murther to adultery,
And with my sword give up his years to death.

DUCHESS
Why, now thou'rt sociable! Let's in and feast.
Loud'st music sound: pleasure is banquet's guest.

[Loud music.] Exeunt.

DUKE
I cannot brook--

[Vindici stabs the Duke, who dies.]

VINDICI
The brook is turn'd to blood.

HIPPOLITO
Thanks to loud music.

VINDICI
'Twas our friend indeed:
'Tis state in music for a duke to bleed.
The dukedom wants a head, tho' yet unknown;
As fast as they peep up, let's cut 'em down.

Exeunt.

[III.vi. The prison]

Enter the Duchess' two sons, Ambitioso and Supervacuo.

AMBITIOSO
Was not this execution rarely plotted?
We are the duke's sons now.

SUPERVACUO
Ay, you may thank my policy for that.

AMBITIOSO
Your policy for what?

SUPERVACUO
Why, was 't not my invention, brother,
To slip the judges, and in lesser compass,
Did not I draw the model of his death,
Advising you to sudden officers
And e'en extemporal execution?

AMBITIOSO
Heart, 'twas a thing I thought on too.

SUPERVACUO
You thought on't too! 'Sfoot, slander not your thoughts
With glorious untruth! I know 'twas from you.

AMBITIOSO
Sir, I say 'twas in my head.

[SUPERVACUO]
Ay, like your brains then,
Ne'er to come out as long as you liv'd.

AMBITIOSO
You'd have the honour on't, forsooth, that your wit
Led him to the scaffold.

SUPERVACUO
Since it is my due,
I'll publish 't, but I'll ha't in spite of you.

AMBITIOSO
Methinks y'are much too bold; you should a little
Remember us, brother, next to be honest duke.

SUPERVACUO
Ay, it shall be as easy for you to be duke
As to be honest, and that's never, i'faith.

AMBITIOSO
Well, cold he is by this time, and because
We're both ambitious, be it our amity,
And let the glory be shar'd equally.

SUPERVACUO
I am content to that.

AMBITIOSO
This night our younger brother shall out of prison;
I have a trick.

SUPERVACUO
A trick? Prithee, what is't?

AMBITIOSO
We'll get him out by a wile.

SUPERVACUO
Prithee, what wile?

AMBITIOSO
No, sir, you shall not know it till 't be done,
For then you'd swear 'twere yours.

[Enter an Officer, holding a severed head.]

SUPERVACUO
How now, what's he?

AMBITIOSO
One of the officers.

SUPERVACUO
Desired news.

AMBITIOSO
How now, my friend?

OFFICER
My lords, under your pardon, I am allotted
To that desertless office, to present you
With the yet bleeding head.

SUPERVACUO
[Aside to Ambitioso] Ha, ha, excellent!

AMBITIOSO
[Aside to Supervacuo] All's sure our own: brother, canst weep, think,st thou?
'Twould grace our flattery much; think of some dame:
'Twill teach thee to dissemble.

SUPERVACUO
[*Aside to Ambitioso*] I have thought;
Now for yourself.

AMBITIOSO
Our sorrows are so fluent,
Our eyes o'erflow our tongues; words spoke in tears
Are like the murmurs of the waters; the sound
Is loudly heard, but cannot be distinguish'd.

SUPERVACUO
How died he, pray?

OFFICER
Oh, full of rage and spleen!

SUPERVACUO
He died most valiantly then; we're glad to hear it.

OFFICER
We could not woo him once to pray.

AMBITIOSO
He show'd himself a gentleman in that:
Give him his due.

OFFICER
But in the stead of prayer,
He drew forth oaths.

SUPERVACUO
Then did he pray, dear heart,
Although you understood him not.

OFFICER
My lords,
E'en at his last, with pardon be it spoke,
He curs'd you both.

SUPERVACUO
He curs'd us? 'Las, good soul!

AMBITIOSO
It was not in our powers, but the duke's pleasure.

[*Aside to Supervacuo*] Finely dissembled a' both sides. Sweet fate,
Oh, happy opportunity!

Enter Lussurioso.

LUSSURIOSO
Now, my lords.

[AMBITIOSO, SUPERVACUO]
Oh!

LUSSURIOSO
Why do you shun me, brothers?
You may come nearer now;
The savour of the prison has forsook me.
I thank such kind lords as yourselves, I'm free.

AMBITIOSO
Alive!

SUPERVACUO
In health!

AMBITIOSO
Releas'd!
We were both e'en amaz'd with joy to see it.

LUSSURIOSO
I am much to thank you.

SUPERVACUO
Faith, we spar'd no tongue unto my lord the duke.

AMBITIOSO
I know your delivery, brother,
Had not been half so sudden but for us.

SUPERVACUO
Oh, how we pleaded!

LUSSURIOSO
Most deserving brothers,
In my best studies I will think of it.

Exit Lussurioso.

AMBITIOSO
Oh, death and vengeance!

SUPERVACUO
Hell and torments!

AMBITIOSO
Slave, cam'st thou to delude us?

OFFICER
Delude you, my lords?

SUPERVACUO
Ay, villain, where's this head now?

OFFICER
Why, here, my lord.
Just after his delivery, you both came
With warrant from the duke to behead your brother.

AMBITIOSO
Ay, our brother, the duke's son.

OFFICER
The duke's son,
My lord, had his release before you came.

AMBITIOSO
Whose head's that then?

OFFICER
His whom you left command for, your own brother's.

AMBITIOSO
Our brother's? Oh, furies!

SUPERVACUO
Plagues!

AMBITIOSO
Confusions!

SUPERVACUO
Darkness!

AMBITIOSO
Devils!

SUPERVACUO
Fell it out so accursedly?

AMBITIOSO
So damnedly?

SUPERVACUO
Villain, I'll brain thee with it!

OFFICER
Oh, my good lord!

[Exit Officer, running.]

SUPERVACUO
The devil overtake thee!

AMBITIOSO
Oh, fatal!

SUPERVACUO
Oh, prodigious to our bloods!

AMBITIOSO
Did we dissemble?

SUPERVACUO
Did we make our tears women for thee?

AMBITIOSO
Laugh and rejoice for thee?

SUPERVACUO
Bring warrant for thy death?

AMBITIOSO
Mock off thy head?

SUPERVACUO
You had a trick, you had a wile, forsooth!

AMBITIOSO
A murrain meet 'em! There's none of these wiles

That ever come to good: I see now
There is nothing sure in mortality but mortality.
Well, no more words; shalt be reveng'd, i'faith.
Come, throw off clouds now, brother, think of vengeance
And deeper-settled hate. Sirrah, sit fast:
We'll pull down all, but thou shalt down at last.

Exeunt.

IV.i. [The palace]

Enter Lussurioso with Hippolito.

LUSSURIOSO
Hippolito.

HIPPOLITO
My lord, has your good lordship
Ought to command me in?

LUSSURIOSO
I prithee leave us.

HIPPOLITO
[*Aside*] How's this? Come and leave us?

LUSSURIOSO
Hippolito.

HIPPOLITO
Your honour,
I stand ready for any duteous employment.

LUSSURIOSO
Heart, what mak'st thou here?

HIPPOLITO
[*Aside*] A pretty, lordly humour:
He bids me to be present, to depart;
Something has stung his honour.

LUSSURIOSO
Be nearer, draw nearer:
Ye are not so good, methinks; I'm angry with you.

HIPPOLITO
With me, my lord? I'm angry with myself for't.

LUSSURIOSO
You did prefer a goodly fellow to me.
'Twas wittily elected, 'twas; I thought
H'ad been a villain, and he proves a knave,
To me a knave.

HIPPOLITO
I chose him for the best, my lord.
'Tis much my sorrow if neglect in him,
Breed discontent in you.

LUSSURIOSO
Neglect? 'Twas will! Judge of it:
Firmly to tell of an incredible act,
Not to be thought, less to be spoken of,
'Twixt my stepmother and the bastard, oh,
Incestuous sweets between 'em!

HIPPOLITO
Fie, my lord!

LUSSURIOSO
I, in kind loyalty to my father's forehead,
Made this a desperate arm, and in that fury
Committed treason on the lawful bed,
And with my sword e'en [ras'd] my father's bosom,
For which I was within a stroke of death.

HIPPOLITO
Alack, I'm sorry.

Enter Vindici [disguised as Piato].

[*Aside*] 'Sfoot, just upon the stroke
Jars in my brother; 'twill be villainous music.

VINDICI
My honoured lord.

LUSSURIOSO
Away! Prithee forsake us;
Hereafter we'll not know thee.

VINDICI
Not know me, my lord? Your lordship cannot choose.

LUSSURIOSO
Be gone, I say: thou art a false knave.

VINDICI
Why, the easier to be known, my lord.

LUSSURIOSO
Push, I shall prove too bitter with a word,
Make thee a perpetual prisoner,
And lay this ironage upon thee!

VINDICI
Mum,
For there's a doom would make a woman dumb.
[*Aside*] Missing the bastard, next him, the wind's come about;
Now 'tis my brother's turn to stay, mine to go out.

Exit Vindici.

LUSSURIOSO
H'as greatly mov'd me.

HIPPOLITO
Much to blame, i'faith.

LUSSURIOSO
But I'll recover to his ruin: 'twas told me lately,
I know not whether falsely, that you'd a brother.

HIPPOLITO
Who I? Yes, my good lord, I have a brother.

LUSSURIOSO
How chance the court ne'er saw him? Of what nature?
How does he apply his hours?

HIPPOLITO
Faith, to curse fates,
Who, as he thinks, ordain'd him to be poor,
Keeps at home full of want and discontent.

LUSSURIOSO
There's hope in him, for discontent and want
Is the best clay to mould a villain of.
Hippolito, wish him repair to us,
If there be ought in him to please our blood;
For thy sake we'll advance him and build fair
His meanest fortunes, for it is in us
To rear up towers from cottages.

HIPPOLITO
It is so, my lord, he will attend your honour;
But he's a man in whom much melancholy dwells.

LUSSURIOSO
Why, the better; bring him to court.

HIPPOLITO
With willingness and speed.
[*Aside*] Whom he cast off e'en now must now succeed.
Brother, disguise must off;
In thine own shape now I'll prefer thee to him:
How strangely does himself work to undo him.

Exit.

LUSSURIOSO
This fellow will come fitly; he shall kill
That other slave that did abuse my spleen
And made it swell to treason. I have put
Much of my heart into him; he must die.
He that knows great men's secrets and proves slight,
That man ne'er lives to see his beard turn white.
Ay, he shall speed him; I'll employ the brother:
Slaves are but nails to drive out one another.
He being of black condition, suitable
To want and ill content, hope of preferment
Will grind him to an edge.

The Nobles enter.

FIRST NOBLE
Good days unto your honour.

LUSSURIOSO
My kind lords, I do return the like.

SECOND NOBLE
Saw you my lord the duke?

LUSSURIOSO
My lord and father, is he from court?

FIRST NOBLE
He's sure from court,
But where, which way his pleasure took, we know not,
Nor can we hear on't.

[Enter the Duke's Gentlemen.]

LUSSURIOSO
Here come those should tell.
Saw you my lord and father?

[FIRST GENTLEMAN]
Not since two hours before noon, my lord,
And then he privately rid forth.

LUSSURIOSO
Oh, he's [rid] forth?

FIRST NOBLE
'Twas wondrous privately.

SECOND NOBLE
There's none i' th' court had any knowledge on't.

LUSSURIOSO
His grace is old and sudden; 'tis no treason
To say the duke my father has a humour
Or such a toy about him: what in us
Would appear light, in him seems virtuous.

[FIRST GENTLEMAN]
'Tis oracle, my lord.

Exeunt.

[IV.ii. The palace]

84

Enter [Vindici] and Hippolito, Vindici out of his disguise.

HIPPOLITO
So, so, all's as it should be; y'are yourself.

VINDICI
How that great villain puts me to my shifts!

HIPPOLITO
He that did lately in disguise reject thee
Shall, now thou art thyself, as much respect thee.

VINDICI
'Twill be the quainter fallacy; but, brother,
'Sfoot, what use will he put me to now, think'st thou?

HIPPOLITO
Nay, you must pardon me in that, I know not:
H'as some employment for you, but what 'tis
He and his secretary, the devil, knows best.

VINDICI
Well, I must suit my tongue to his desires,
What colour soe'er they be, hoping at last
To pile up all my wishes on his breast.

HIPPOLITO
Faith, brother, he himself shows the way.

VINDICI
Now the duke is dead, the realm is clad in clay:
His death being not yet known, under his name
The people still are govern'd. Well, thou his son
Art not long-liv'd; thou shalt not 'joy his death:
To kill thee then, I should most honour thee,
For 'twould stand firm in every man's belief
Thou'st a kind child and only died'st with grief.

HIPPOLITO
You fetch about well, but let's talk in present.
How will you appear in fashion different,
As well as in apparel, to make all things possible?
If you be but once tripp'd, we fall forever.

It is not the least policy to be doubtful;
You must change tongue: familiar was your first.

VINDICI
Why, I'll bear me in some strain of melancholy
And string myself with heavy-sounding wire,
Like such an instrument, that speaks merry
Things sadly.

HIPPOLITO
Then 'tis as I meant:
I gave you out at first in discontent.

VINDICI
I'll turn myself, and then--

[Enter Lussurioso.]

HIPPOLITO
[Aside to Vindici] 'Sfoot, here he comes!
Hast thought upon't?

VINDICI
[Aside to Hippolito] Salute him, fear not me.

LUSSURIOSO
Hippolito.

HIPPOLITO
Your lordship.

LUSSURIOSO
What's he yonder?

HIPPOLITO
'Tis Vindici, my discontented brother,
Whom 'cording to your will I've brought to court.

LUSSURIOSO
Is that thy brother? Beshrew me, a good presence;
I wonder h'as been from the court so long. [To Vindici] Come nearer.

HIPPOLITO
Brother, Lord Lussurioso, the duke['s] son.

[Vindici] snatches off his hat and makes legs to him.

LUSSURIOSO
Be more near to us; welcome, nearer yet.

VINDICI
How don you? God you god den.

LUSSURIOSO
We thank thee.
How strangely such a coarse, homely salute
Shows in the palace, where we greet in fire
Nimble and desperate tongues; should we name
God in a salutation, 'twould ne'er be stood on't. Heaven!
Tell me, what has made thee so melancholy?

VINDICI
Why, going to law.

LUSSURIOSO
Why, will that make a man melancholy?

VINDICI
Yes, to look long upon ink and black buckram: I went me to law in *anno quadregesimo secundo*, and I waded out of it in *anno sextagesimo tertio*.

LUSSURIOSO
What, three and twenty years in law?

VINDICI
I have known those that have been five and fifty, and all about pullen and pigs.

LUSSURIOSO
May it be possible such men should breath,
To vex the terms so much?

VINDICI
'Tis food to some, my lord. There are old men at the present that are so poisoned with the affectation of law-words, having had many suites canvass'd, that their common talk is nothing but Barbary Latin: they cannot so much as pray but in law, that their sins may be remov'd with a writ of error, and their souls fetch'd up to heaven with a *sasarara*.

[LUSSURIOSO]
It seems most strange to me,
Yet all the world meets round in the same bent:
Where the heart's set, there goes the tongue's consent.
How dost apply thy studies, fellow?

VINDICI
Study? Why, to think how a great, rich man lies a-dying, and a poor cobbler
tolls the bell for him; how he cannot depart the world, and see the great chest
stand before him; when he lies speechless, how he will point you readily to all
the boxes; and when he is past all memory, as the gossipsguess, then thinks he
of forfeitures and obligations; nay, when to all men's hearings he whirls and
rattles in the throat, he's busy threat'ning his poor tenants; and this would last
me now some seven years thinking or thereabouts. But I have a conceit a-
coming in picture upon this: I draw it myself, which, i'faith la, I'll present to
your honour; you shall not choose but like it, for your lordship shall give me
nothing for it.

LUSSURIOSO
Nay, you mistake me then,
For I am publish'd bountiful enough;
Let's taste of your conceit.

VINDICI
In picture, my lord?

LUSSURIOSO
Ay, in picture.

VINDICI
Marry, this it is:
"A usuring father to be boiling in hell,
And his son and heir with a whore dancing over him."

HIPPOLITO
[*Aside*] H'as par'd him to the quick.

LUSSURIOSO
The conceit's pretty, i'faith,
But take 't upon my life, 'twill ne'er be lik'd.

VINDICI
No? Why, I'm sure the whore will be lik'd well enough.

HIPPOLITO
[*Aside*] Ay, if she were out a' th' picture, he'd like her then himself.

VINDICI
And as for the son and heir, he shall be an eyesore to no young revellers, for he shall be drawn in cloth-of-gold breeches.

LUSSURIOSO
And thou hast put my meaning in the pockets
And canst not draw that out; my thought was this:
To see the picture of a usuring father
Boiling in hell, our rich men would ne'er like it.

VINDICI
Oh, true, I cry you heartily mercy! I know the reason, for some of 'em had rather be damn'd indeed than damn'd in colours.

LUSSURIOSO
[*Aside*] A parlous melancholy; h'as wit enough
To murder any man, and I'll give him means.--
I think thou art ill-monied.

VINDICI
Money! Ho, ho!
'T 'as been my want so long, 'tis now my scoff.
I've e'en forgot what colour silver's of.

LUSSURIOSO
[*Aside*] It hits as I could wish.

VINDICI
I get good clothes
Of those that dread my humour, and for tableroom,
I feed on those that cannot be rid of me.

LUSSURIOSO
[*Giving him gold*] Somewhat to set thee up withal.

VINDICI
Oh, mine eyes!

LUSSURIOSO
How now, man?

VINDICI
Almost struck blind!
This bright, unusual shine to me seems proud;
I dare not look till the sun be in a cloud.

LUSSURIOSO
[*Aside*] I think I shall affect his melancholy.--
How are they now?

VINDICI
The better for your asking.

LUSSURIOSO
You shall be better yet if you but fasten
Truly on my intent; now y'are both present,
I will unbrace such a close, private villain
Unto your vengeful swords, the like ne'er heard of,
Who hath disgrac'd you much and injur'd us.

HIPPOLITO
Disgraced us, my lord?

LUSSURIOSO
Ay, Hippolito.
I kept it here till now that both your angers
Might meet him at once.

VINDICI
I'm covetous
To know the villain.

LUSSURIOSO
You know him: that slave pander,
Piato, whom we threatened last
With iron's perpetual prisonment.

VINDICI
[*Aside*] All this is I.

HIPPOLITO
Is't he, my lord?

LUSSURIOSO
I'll tell you,
You first preferr'd him to me.

VINDICI
Did you, brother?

HIPPOLITO
I did indeed.

LUSSURIOSO
And the ingrateful villain,
To quit that kindness, strongly wrought with me,
Being as you see a likely man for pleasure,
With jewels to corrupt your virgin sister.

HIPPOLITO
Oh, villain!

VINDICI
He shall surely die that did it.

LUSSURIOSO
Ay, far from thinking any virgin harm,
Especially knowing her to be as chaste
As that part which scarce suffers to be touch'd,
Th' eye would not endure him.

VINDICI
Would you not, my lord?
'Twas wondrous honourably done.

LUSSURIOSO
But with some [fine] frowns kept him out.

VINDICI
Out, slave!

LUSSURIOSO
What did me he but in revenge of that
Went of his own free will to make infirm
Your sister's honour, whom I honour with my soul
For chaste respect, and not prevailing there,
As 'twas but desperate folly to attempt it,
In mere spleen, by the way, waylays your mother,
Whose honour being a coward as it seems
Yielded by little force.

VINDICI
Coward indeed!

LUSSURIOSO
He, proud of their advantage, as he thought,
Brought me these news for happy, but I,
Heaven forgive me for't--

VINDICI
What did your honour?

LUSSURIOSO
In rage push'd him from me,
Trampled beneath his throat, spurn'd him, and bruis'd:
Indeed I was too cruel, to say troth.

HIPPOLITO
Most nobly manag'd.

VINDICI
Has not heaven an ear? Is all lightning wasted?

LUSSURIOSO
If I now were so impatient in a modest cause,
What should you be?

VINDICI
Full mad: he shall not live
To see the moon change.

LUSSURIOSO
He's about the palace;
Hippolito, entice him this way, that thy brother
May take full mark of him.

HIPPOLITO
Heart, that shall not need, my lord,
I can direct him so far.

LUSSURIOSO
Yet for my hate's sake,
Go, wind him this way; I'll see him bleed myself.

HIPPOLITO
[*Taking Vindici aside*] What now, brother?

VINDICI
Nay, e'en what you will: y'are put to't, brother.

HIPPOLITO
An impossible task, I'll swear,
To bring him hither that's already here.

Exit Hippolito.

LUSSURIOSO
Thy name, I have forgot it.

VINDICI
[Vindici], my lord.

LUSSURIOSO
'Tis a good name, that.

VINDICI
Ay, a revenger.

LUSSURIOSO
It does betoken courage: [thou] shouldst be valiant
And kill thine enemies.

VINDICI
That's my hope, my lord.

LUSSURIOSO
This slave is one.

VINDICI
I'll doom him.

LUSSURIOSO
Then I'll praise thee.
Do thou observe me best, and I'll best raise thee.

Enter Hippolito.

VINDICI
Indeed, I thank you.

LUSSURIOSO
Now, Hippolito,
Where's the slave pander?

HIPPOLITO
Your good lordship
Would have a loathsome sight of him, much offensive.
He's not in case now to be seen, my lord;
The worst of all the deadly sins is in him:
That beggarly damnation, drunkenness.

LUSSURIOSO
Then he's a double slave.

VINDICI
[*Aside to Hippolito*] 'Twas well convey'd
Upon a sudden wit.

LUSSURIOSO
What, are you both
Firmly resolv'd? I'll see him dead myself.

VINDICI
Or else let not us live.

LUSSURIOSO
You may direct
Your brother to take note of him.

HIPPOLITO
I shall.

LUSSURIOSO
Rise but in this and you shall never fall.

VINDICI
Your honour's vassals.

LUSSURIOSO
[*Aside*] This was wisely carried.
Deep policy in us makes fools of such:
Then must a slave die when he knows too much.

Exit Lussurioso.

VINDICI
Oh, thou almighty patience, 'tis my wonder
That such a fellow, impudent and wicked,
Should not be cloven as he stood,
Or with a secret wind burst open!
Is there no thunder left, or is't kept up
In stock for heavier vengeance? There it goes!

HIPPOLITO
Brother, we lose ourselves.

VINDICI
But I have found it.
'Twill hold, 'tis sure; thanks, thanks to any spirit
That mingled it 'mongst my inventions!

HIPPOLITO
What is't?

VINDICI
'Tis sound and good, thou shalt partake it:
I'm hir'd to kill myself.

HIPPOLITO
True.

VINDICI
Prithee mark it:
And the old duke being dead but not convey'd,
For he's already miss'd too, and you know
Murder will peep out of the closest husk.

HIPPOLITO
Most true.

VINDICI
What say you then to this device,
If we dress'd up the body of the duke?

HIPPOLITO
In that disguise of yours.

VINDICI
Y'are quick, y'ave reach'd it.

HIPPOLITO
I like it wondrously.

VINDICI
And being in drink, as you have publish'd him,
To lean him on his elbow, as if sleep had caught him,
Which claims most interest in such sluggy men.

HIPPOLITO
Good yet, but here's a doubt:
[We], thought by th' duke's son to kill that pander,
Shall when he is known be thought to kill the duke.

VINDICI
Neither. Oh, thanks, it is substantial!
For that disguise being on him, which I wore,
It will be thought I, which he calls the pander,
Did kill the duke and fled away in his apparel,
Leaving him so disguis'd to avoid swift pursuit.

HIPPOLITO
Firmer and firmer.

VINDICI
Nay, doubt not 'tis in grain;
I warrant it hold colour.

HIPPOLITO
Let's about it.

VINDICI
But, by the way too, now I think on't, brother,
Let's conjure that base devil out of our mother.

Exeunt.

[IV.iii. The palace]

Enter the Duchess arm in arm with the bastard [Spurio]; he seemeth lasciviously to her. After them, enter Supervacuo, running with a rapier, his brother [Ambitioso] stops him.

SPURIO
Madam, unlock yourself; should it be seen,
Your arm would be suspected.

DUCHESS
Who is't that dares suspect, or this or these?
May not we deal our favours where we please?

SPURIO
I'm confident you may.

Exeunt [Duchess and Spurio].

AMBITIOSO
'Sfoot, brother, hold!

SUPERVACUO
Woult let the bastard shame us?

AMBITIOSO
Hold, hold, brother;
There's fitter time than now.

SUPERVACUO
Now, when I see it!

AMBITIOSO
'Tis too much seen already.

SUPERVACUO
Seen and known,
The nobler she's, the baser is she grown.

AMBITIOSO
If she were bent lasciviously, the fault
Of mighty women that sleep soft. Oh, death,
Must she needs choose such an unequal sinner
To make all worse?

SUPERVACUO
A bastard, the duke's bastard!
Shame heap'd on shame!

AMBITIOSO
Oh, our disgrace!
Most women have small [waist] the world throughout,
But [their] desires are thousand miles about.

SUPERVACUO
Come, stay not here, let's after and prevent,
Or else they'll sin faster than we'll repent.

[IV.iv. Vindici's house]

*Enter [Vindici] and Hippolito bringing out [their] mother [Gratiana], one by one
shoulder, and the other by the other, with daggers in their hands.*

VINDICI
Oh, thou for whom no name is bad enough!

[GRATIANA]
What means my sons? What, will you murder me?

VINDICI
Wicked, unnatural parent!

HIPPOLITO
Fiend of women!

[GRATIANA]
Oh! Are sons turn'd monsters? Help!

VINDICI
In vain.

[GRATIANA]
Are you so barbarous to set iron nipples
Upon the breast that gave you suck?

VINDICI
That breast
Is turned to quarled poison.

[GRATIANA]
Cut not your days for't: am not I your mother?

VINDICI
Thou dost usurp that title now by fraud,
For in that shell of mother breeds a bawd.

[GRATIANA]
A bawd? Oh, name far loathsomer than hell!

HIPPOLITO
It should be so, knew'st thou thy office well.

[GRATIANA]
I hate it!

VINDICI
Ah, is't possible, you powers on high,
That women should dissemble when they die?

[GRATIANA]
Dissemble!

VINDICI
Did not the duke's son direct
A fellow of the world's condition hither,
That did corrupt all that was good in thee,
Made thee uncivilly forget thyself,
And work our sister to his lust?

[GRATIANA]
Who, I?
That had been monstrous! I defy that man
For any such intent: none lives so pure
But shall be soil'd with slander.
Good son, believe it not.

VINDICI
Oh, I'm in doubt,
Whether I'm myself or no.
Stay, let me look again upon this face.
Who shall be sav'd when mothers have no grace?

HIPPOLITO
'Twould make one half despair.

VINDICI
I was the man.
Defy me now? Let's see do't modestly.

[GRATIANA]
Oh, hell unto my soul!

VINDICI
In that disguise, I sent from the duke's son,

Tried you, you, and found you base metal
As any villain might have done.

[GRATIANA]
Oh, no,
No tongue but yours could have bewitch'd me so.

VINDICI
Oh, nimble in damnation, quick in tune;
There is no devil could strike fire so soon!
I am confuted in a word.

[GRATIANA]
Oh, sons,
Forgive me; to myself I'll prove more true:
You that should honour me, I kneel to you.

VINDICI
A mother to give aim to her own daughter.

HIPPOLITO
True, brother, how far beyond nature 'tis,
Tho' many mothers do't.

VINDICI
Nay, and you draw tears once, go you to bed.
Wet will make iron blush and change to red:
Brother, it rains, 'twill spoil your dagger; house it.

HIPPOLITO
'Tis done.

VINDICI
I'faith, 'tis a sweet shower; it does much good.
The fruitful grounds and meadows of her soul
Has been long dry: pour down thou blessed dew.
Rise, mother; troth, this shower has made you higher.

[GRATIANA]
Oh, you heavens!
Take this infectious spot out of my soul;
I'll rinse it in seven waters of mine eyes.
Make my tears salt enough to taste of grace.

To weep is to our sex naturally given,
But to weep truly, that's a gift from heaven.

VINDICI
Nay, I'll kiss you now. Kiss her, brother.
Let's marry her to our souls, wherein's no lust,
And honourably love her.

HIPPOLITO
Let it be.

VINDICI
For honest women are so [seld] and rare,
'Tis good to cherish those poor few that are.
Oh, you of easy wax, do but imagine
Now the disease has left you, how leprously
That office would have cling'd unto your forehead.
All mothers that had any graceful hue
Would have worn masks to hide their face at you;
It would have grown to this: at your foul name
Green-colour'd maids would have turn'd red with shame.

HIPPOLITO
And then our sister, full of hire and baseness--

VINDICI
There had been boiling lead again.
The duke's son's great concubine!
A drab of state, a cloth-a'-silver slut,
To have her train borne up and her soul trail
I' th' dirt: great!

HIPPOLITO
To be miserably great; rich,
To be eternally wretched.

VINDICI
Oh, common madness!
Ask but the thriving'st harlot in cold blood,
She'd give the world to make her honour good.
Perhaps you'll say but only to th' duke's son
In private; why, she first begins with one
Who afterward to thousand proves a whore:
"Break ice in one place, it will crack in more."

[GRATIANA]
Most certainly applied.

HIPPOLITO
Oh, brother, you forget our business.

VINDICI
And well rememb'red; joy's a subtle elf:
I think man's happiest when he forgets himself.
Farewell, once dried, now holy-wat'red mead;
Our hearts wear feathers that before wore lead.

[GRATIANA]
I'll give you this, that one I never knew
Plead better for and 'gainst the devil than you.

VINDICI
You make me proud on't.

HIPPOLITO
Commend us in all virtue to our sister.

VINDICI
Ay, for the love of heaven, to that true maid.

[GRATIANA]
With my best words.

VINDICI
Why, that was motherly said.

Exeunt [Vindici and Hippolito].

[GRATIANA]
I wonder now what fury did transport me?
I feel good thoughts begin to settle in me.
Oh, with what forehead can I look on her
Whose honour I've so impiously beset?

[Enter Castiza.]

And here she comes.

CASTIZA
Now, mother, you have wrought with me so strongly

That what for my advancement, as to calm
The trouble of your tongue: I am content.

[GRATIANA]
Content to what?

CASTIZA
To do as you have wish'd me,
To prostitute my breast to the duke's son,
And to put myself to common usury.

[GRATIANA]
I hope you will not so!

CASTIZA
Hope you I will not?
That's not the hope you look to be saved in.

[GRATIANA]
Truth, but it is.

CASTIZA
Do not deceive yourself;
I am as you e'en out of marble wrought.
What would you now? Are ye not pleas'd yet with me?
You shall not wish me to be more lascivious
Than I intend to be.

[GRATIANA]
Strike not me cold.

CASTIZA
How often have you charg'd me on your blessing
To be a cursed woman! When you knew
Your blessing had no force to make me lewd,
You laid your curse upon me. That did more;
The mother's curse is heavy: where that fights,
Suns set in storm and daughters lose their lights.

[GRATIANA]
Good child, dear maid, if there be any spark
Of heavenly intellectual fire within thee,
Oh, let my breath revive it to a flame!
Put not all out with woman's wilful follies.

I am recover'd of that foul disease
That haunts too many mothers. Kind, forgive me;
Make me not sick in health: if then
My words prevail'd when they were wickedness,
How much more now when they are just and good?

CASTIZA
I wonder what you mean. Are not you she
For whose infect persuasions I could scarce
Kneel out my prayers, and had much ado
In three hours reading to untwist so much
Of the black serpent as you wound about me?

[GRATIANA]
'Tis unfruitful, held tedious to repeat what's past;
I'm now your present mother.

CASTIZA
Push, now 'tis too late.

[GRATIANA]
Bethink again, thou know'st not what thou sayst.

CASTIZA
No? Deny advancement, treasure, the duke's son?

[GRATIANA]
Oh, see,
I spoke those words, and now they poison me!
What will the deed do then?
Advancement? True, as high as shame can pitch.
For treasure, whoe'er knew a harlot rich,
Or could build by the purchase of her sin
An hospital to keep their bastards in?
The duke's son! Oh, when women are young courtiers,
They are sure to be old beggars!
To know the miseries most harlots taste,
Thou'dst wish thyself unborn when thou art unchaste.

CASTIZA
Oh, mother, let me twine about your neck,
And kiss you till my soul melt on your lips:
I did but this to try you.

[GRATIANA]
Oh, speak truth!

CASTIZA
Indeed, I did not, for no tongue has force
To alter me from honest.
If maidens would, men's words could have no power.
A virgin honour is a crystal tower,
Which being weak is guarded with good spirits:
Until she basely yields no ill inherits.

[GRATIANA]
Oh, happy child! Faith and thy birth hath saved me.
'Mongst thousands daughters happiest of all others!
[Be] thou a glass for maids, and I for mothers.

Exeunt.

[V.i. A room in the palace]

Enter [Vindici] and Hippolito [with the Duke's corpse in Piato's clothes, which they prop up in chair].

VINDICI
So, so, he leans well; take heed you wake him not, brother.

HIPPOLITO
I warrant you, my life for yours.

VINDICI
That's a good lay, for I must kill myself!
Brother, that's I: that sits for me, do you mark it?
And I must stand ready here to make away myself yonder: I must sit to be
kill'd, and stand to kill myself. I could vary it not so little as thrice over again,
't 'as some eight returns like Michaelmas Term.

HIPPOLITO
That's enow, a' conscience.

VINDICI
But, sirrah, does the duke's son come single?

HIPPOLITO
No, there's the hell on't, his faith's too feeble to go alone; he brings flesh-
flies after him that will buzz against suppertime and hum for his coming out.

VINDICI
Ah, the fly-flop of vengeance beat 'em to pieces! Here was the sweetest
occasion, the fittest hour, to have made my revenge familiar with him, show
him the body of the duke his father, and how quaintly he died like
a politician in huggermugger, made no man acquainted with it, and
incatastrophe slain him over his father's breast, and oh, I'm mad to lose such
a sweet opportunity!

HIPPOLITO
Nay, push, prithee be content! There's no remedy present; may not hereafter
times open in as fair faces as this?

VINDICI
They may if they can paint so well.

HIPPOLITO
Come, now to avoid all suspicion, let's forsake this room, and be going to
meet the duke's son.

VINDICI
Content, I'm for any weather.

Enter Lussurioso.

Heart, step close, here he comes!

HIPPOLITO
My honour'd lord?

LUSSURIOSO
Oh, me; you both present?

VINDICI
E'en newly, my lord, just as your lordship enter'd now; about this place we
had notice given he should be, but in some loathsome plight or other.

HIPPOLITO
Came your honour private?

LUSSURIOSO
Private enough for this: only a few
Attend my coming out.

HIPPOLITO
[*Aside*] Death rot those few!

LUSSURIOSO
Stay, yonder's the slave.

VINDICI
Mass, there's the slave indeed, my lord!
[*Aside*] 'Tis a good child, he calls his father slave.

LUSSURIOSO
Ay, that's the villain, the damn'd villain: softly,
Tread easy.

VINDICI
Puh, I warrant you, my lord,
We'll stifle in our breaths.

LUSSURIOSO
That will do well.
[*Aside*] Base rogue, thou sleepest thy last; 'tis policy
To have him kill'd in's sleep, for if he wak'd
He would betray all to them.

VINDICI
But, my lord--

LUSSURIOSO
Ha, what sayst?

VINDICI
Shall we kill him now he's drunk?

LUSSURIOSO
Ay, best of all.

VINDICI
Why, then he will ne'er live to be sober.

LUSSURIOSO
No matter, let him reel to hell.

VINDICI
But being so full of liquor, I fear he will put out all the fire--

LUSSURIOSO
Thou art a mad beast.

VINDICI
And leave none to warm your lordship's golls withal,
For he that dies drunk falls into hellfire
Like a bucket a' water, qush, qush.

LUSSURIOSO
Come, be ready, nake your swords; think of your wrongs:
This slave has injur'd you.

VINDICI
[*Aside*] Troth, so he has,
And he has paid well for't.

LUSSURIOSO
Meet with him now.

VINDICI
You'll bear us out, my lord?

LUSSURIOSO
Puh, am I a lord for nothing think you? Quickly, now.

VINDICI
Sa, sa, sa! [*Stabs the corpse.*] Thump, there he lies.

LUSSURIOSO
Nimbly done. Ha? Oh, villains, murderers,
'Tis the old duke my father!

VINDICI
That's a jest.

LUSSURIOSO
What stiff and cold already?
Oh, pardon me to call you from your names;
'Tis none of your deed: that villain Piato,
Whom you thought now to kill, has murder'd him
And left him thus disguis'd.

HIPPOLITO
And not unlikely.

VINDICI
Oh, rascal! Was he not asham'd
To put the duke into a greasy doublet?

LUSSURIOSO
He has been cold and stiff who knows how long?

VINDICI
[*Aside*] Marry, that do I!

LUSSURIOSO
No words, I pray, of anything intended.

VINDICI
Oh, my lord!

HIPPOLITO
I would fain have your lordship think that we have small reason to prate.

LUSSURIOSO
Faith, thou sayst true; I'll forthwith send to court
For all the nobles, bastard, duchess, all,
How here by miracle we found him dead,
And in his raiment that foul villain fled.

VINDICI
That will be the best way, my lord, to clear us all: let's cast about to be clear.

LUSSURIOSO
Ho, Nencio, Sordido, and the rest!

Enter all [Lussurioso's attendants].

[SORDIDO]
My lord.

[NENCIO]
My lord.

LUSSURIOSO
Be witnesses of a strange spectacle:
Choosing for private conference that sad room,
We found the duke my father 'geal'd in blood.

[SORDIDO]
My lord, the duke! Run, hie thee, Nencio,
Startle the court by signifying so much.

[Exit Nencio.]

VINDICI
[*Aside to Hippolito*] Thus much by wit a deep revenger can:
When murder's known, to be the clearest man.
We're fardest off, and with as bold an eye
Survey his body as the standers-by.

LUSSURIOSO
My royal father, too basely let blood
By a malevolent slave!

HIPPOLITO
[*Aside to Vindici*] Hark, he calls thee slave again.

VINDICI
[*Aside to Hippolito*] Ha's lost, he may.

LUSSURIOSO
Oh, sight, look hither! See, his lips are gnawn with poison!

VINDICI
How! His lips? By th' mass, they be!

LUSSURIOSO
Oh, villain! Oh, rogue! Oh, slave! Oh, rascal!

HIPPOLITO
[*Aside*] Oh, good deceit! He quits him with like terms.

[*Enter Ambitioso, Supervacuo, Spurio, Duchess, the Duke's Gentlemen, Nobles, and guards.*]

FIRST NOBLE
Where?

SECOND NOBLE
Which way?

AMBITIOSO
Over what roof hangs this prodigious comet
In deadly fire?

LUSSURIOSO
Behold, behold, my lords:
The duke my father's murder'd by a vassal
That owes this habit, and here left disguis'd.

DUCHESS
My lord and husband!

SECOND NOBLE
Reverend majesty!

FIRST NOBLE
I have seen these clothes often attending on him.

VINDICI
[*Aside*] That nobleman has been i' th' country, for he does not lie.

SUPERVACUO
[*Aside to Ambitioso*] Learn of our mother; let's dissemble too.
I am glad he's vanish'd; so I hope are you.

AMBITIOSO
[*Aside to Supervacuo*] Ay, you may take my word for't.

SPURIO
[*Aside*] Old Dad dead?
Ay, one of his cast sins will send the fates
Most hearty commendations by his own son.
I'll tug the new stream till strength be done.

LUSSURIOSO
Where be those two that did affirm to us
My lord the duke was privately rid forth?

FIRST GENTLEMAN
Oh, pardon us, my lords, he gave that charge
Upon our lives if he were miss'd at court
To answer so; he rode not anywhere,
We left him private with that fellow here.

VINDICI
[*Aside*] Confirm'd.

LUSSURIOSO
Oh heavens, that false charge was his death!
Impudent beggars, durst you to our face,
Maintain such a false answer? Bear him straight
To execution.

FIRST GENTLEMAN
My lord!

LUSSURIOSO
Urge me no more.
In this excuse may be call'd half the murther.

VINDICI
[*Aside*] You've sentenc'd well.

LUSSURIOSO
Away, see it be done.

[*Exit the First Gentleman, guarded.*]

VINDICI
[*Aside*] Could you not stick? See what confession doth.
Who would not lie when men are hang'd for truth?

HIPPOLITO
[*Aside to Vindici*] Brother, how happy is our vengeance?

VINDICI
[*Aside to Hippolito*] Why, it hits,
Past the apprehension of indifferent wits.

LUSSURIOSO
My lord, let post-horse be sent
Into all places to entrap the villain.

VINDICI
[*Aside*] Post-horse? Ha, ha!

[FIRST] NOBLE
My lord, we're something bold to know our duty.
You father's accidentally departed;
The titles that were due to him meet you.

LUSSURIOSO
Meet me? I'm not at leisure, my good lord;
I've many griefs to dispatch out a' th' way.
[*Aside*] Welcome, sweet titles!--Talk to me, my lords,
Of sepulchers and mighty emperors' bones,
That's thought for me.

VINDICI
[*Aside*] So, one may see by this
How foreign markets go:
Courtiers have feet a' th' nines and tongues a' th' twelves;
They flatter dukes and dukes flatter themselves.

[FIRST] NOBLE
My lord, it is your shine must comfort us.

LUSSURIOSO
Alas, I shine in tears like the sun in April.

[FIRST] NOBLE
You're now my lord's grace.

LUSSURIOSO
My lord's grace? I perceive you'll have it so.

[FIRST] NOBLE
'Tis but your own.

LUSSURIOSO
Then heavens give me grace to be so.

VINDICI
[*Aside*] He prays well for himself.

[FIRST] NOBLE
Madam, all sorrows
Must run their circles into joys; no doubt but time
Will make the murderer bring forth himself.

VINDICI
[*Aside*] He were an ass then, i'faith.

[FIRST] NOBLE
In the mean season,
Let us bethink the latest funeral honours
Due to the duke's cold body, and withal,
Calling to memory our new happiness,
Spread in his royal son: lords, gentlemen,
Prepare for revels.

VINDICI
[*Aside*] Revels!

NOBLE
Time hath several falls.
Griefs lift up joys, feasts put down funerals.

LUSSURIOSO
Come then, my lords, my favours to you all.
[*Aside*] The duchess is suspected foully bent;
I'll begin dukedom with her banishment.

Exeunt Duke [Lussurioso], Nobles, [Gentlemen, Attendants,] and Duchess.

HIPPOLITO
[*Aside to Vindici*] Revels!

VINDICI
[*Aside to Hippolito*] Ay, that's the word; we are firm yet:
Strike one strain more and then we crown our wit.

Exeunt brothers [Vindici and Hippolito].

SPURIO
Well, have the fairest mark, so said the duke when he begot me,
And if I miss his heart or near about,
Then have at any: a bastard scorns to be out.

[Exit Spurio.]

SUPERVACUO
Not'st thou that Spurio, brother?

[AMBITIOSO]
Yes, I note him to our shame.

SUPERVACUO
He shall not live; his hair shall not grow much longer: in this time of revels, tricks may be set afoot. Seest thou yon new moon? It shall out-live the new duke by much; this hand shall dispossess him, then we're mighty.
A masque is treason's license; that build upon:
'Tis murder's best face when a vizard's on.

Exit [Supervacuo].

AMBITIOSO
Is't so? ['Tis] very good.

And do you think to be duke then, kind brother?
I'll see fair play: drop one and there lies t'other.

Exit Ambitioso.

[V.ii. Vindici's house]

Enter [Vindici] and Hippolito, with Piero and other Lords.

VINDICI
My lords, be all of music; strike old griefs into other countries
That flow in too much milk and have faint livers,
Not daring to stab home their discontents:
Let our hid flames break out as fire, as lightning,
To blast this villainous dukedom vex'd with sin;
Wind up your souls to their full height again.

PIERO
How?

FIRST LORD
Which way?

THIRD LORD
Any way: our wrongs are such,
We cannot justly be reveng'd too much.

VINDICI
You shall have all enough. Revels are toward,
And those few nobles that have long suppress'd you
Are busied to the furnishing of a masque,
And do affect to make a pleasant tale on't.
The masquing suits are fashioning; now comes in
That which must glad us all: we to take pattern
Of all those suits, the colour, trimming, fashion,
E'en to an undistinguish'd hair almost,
Then ent'ring first, observing the true form,
Within a strain or two we shall find leisure
To steal our swords out handsomely,
And when they think their pleasure sweet and good,
In midst of all their joys, they shall sigh blood.

PIERO
Weightily, effectually.

THIRD LORD
Before the t'other masquers come.

VINDICI
We're gone, all done and past.

PIERO
But how for the duke's guard?

VINDICI
Let that alone;
By one and one their strengths shall be drunk down.

HIPPOLITO
There are five hundred gentlemen in the action
That will apply themselves and not stand idle.

PIERO
Oh, let us hug your bosoms!

VINDICI
Come, my lords,
Prepare for deeds; let other times have words.

Exeunt.

[V.iii. The palace banqueting hall]

In a dumb show, the possessing of the young duke [Lussurioso] with all his Nobles.
Then sounding music, a furnish'd table is brought forth; then enters the duke [Lussurioso]
and his [three] Nobles to the banquet. A blazing star appeareth.

[FIRST] NOBLE
Many harmonious hours and choicest pleasures
Fill up the royal numbers of your years.

LUSSURIOSO
My lords, we're pleas'd to thank you [*aside*] tho' we know
'Tis but your duty now to wish it so.

[FIRST] NOBLE
That shine makes us all happy.

THIRD NOBLE
[*Aside*] His grace frowns?

SECOND NOBLE
[*Aside*] Yet we must say he smiles.

FIRST NOBLE
[*Aside*] I think we must.

LUSSURIOSO
[*Aside*] That foul, incontinent duchess we have banish'd;
The bastard shall not live: after these revels
I'll begin strange ones; he and the stepsons
Shall pay their lives for the first subsidies.
We must not frown so soon, else 't 'ad been now.

FIRST NOBLE
My gracious lord, please you prepare for pleasure:
The masque is not far off.

LUSSURIOSO
We are for pleasure.
[*To the comet*] Beshrew thee, what art thou mad'st me start?
Thou hast committed treason: a blazing star!

FIRST NOBLE
A blazing star? Oh, where, my lord?

LUSSURIOSO
Spy out!

SECOND NOBLE
See, see, my lords: a wondrous, dreadful one.

LUSSURIOSO
I am not pleas'd at that ill-knotted fire,
That bushing, flaring star. Am not I duke?
It should not quake me now: had it appear'd
Before it, I might then have justly fear'd;
But yet they say, whom art and learning weds,
When stars [wear] locks, they threaten great men's heads.
Is it so? You are read, my lords.

FIRST NOBLE
May it please your grace,
It shows great anger.

LUSSURIOSO
That does not please our grace.

SECOND NOBLE
Yet here's the comfort, my lord: many times
When it seems most, it threatens fardest off.

LUSSURIOSO
Faith, and I think so too.

FIRST NOBLE
Beside, my lord,
You're gracefully establish'd with the loves
Of all your subjects: and for natural death,
I hope it will be threescore years a-coming.

LUSSURIOSO
True. No more but threescore years?

FIRST NOBLE
Fourscore I hope, my lord.

SECOND NOBLE
And fivescore, I.

THIRD NOBLE
But 'tis my hope, my lord, you shall ne'er die.

LUSSURIOSO
Give me thy hand; these others I rebuke.
He that hopes so is fittest for a duke.
Thou shalt sit next me; take your places, lords:
We're ready now for sports; let 'em set on.
[*To the comet*] You thing, we shall forget you quite anon!

THIRD NOBLE
I hear 'em coming, my lord.

Enter the Masque of Revengers: the two brothers [Vindici and Hippolito] and two Lords more.

LUSSURIOSO
Ah, 'tis well.
[*Aside*] Brothers and bastard, you dance next in hell.

The Revengers dance. At the end, steal out their swords and these four kill the four at the table in their chairs. It thunders.

VINDICI
Mark thunder?
Dost know thy cue, thou big-voic'd crier?
Dukes' groans are thunder's watchwords.

HIPPOLITO
So, my lords, you have enough.

VINDICI
Come, let's away, no ling'ring.

HIPPOLITO
Follow, go.

Exeunt [Hippolito and the two lords].

VINDICI
No power is angry when the lustful die;
When thunder claps, heaven likes the tragedy.

Exit Vindici. Enter the other masque of intended murderers: stepsons [Ambitioso, Supervacuo], bastard [Spurio], and a Fourth Man [Ambitioso's henchman], coming in dancing; the duke [Lussurioso] recovers a little in voice and groans, calls, "A guard, treason," at which they all start out of their measure, and turning towards the table, they find them all to be murdered.

LUSSURIOSO
Oh, oh!

SPURIO
Whose groan was that?

LUSSURIOSO
Treason, a guard!

AMBITIOSO
How now? All murder'd!

SUPERVACUO
Murder'd!

FOURTH MAN
And those his nobles?

AMBITIOSO
Here's a labour sav'd:
I thought to have sped him. 'Sblood, how came this?

[SUPERVACUO]
Then I proclaim myself: now I am duke.

AMBITIOSO
Thou duke! Brother, thou liest.

[Kills Supervacuo.]

SPURIO
Slave, so dost thou!

[Kills Ambitioso.]

FOURTH MAN
Base villain, hast thou slain my lord and master?

[Kills Spurio.] Enter the first men [Vindici, Hippolito, the two Lords].

VINDICI
Pistols, treason, murder! Help, guard my lord the duke!

[Enter Antonio, guards.]

HIPPOLITO
Lay hold upon this traitor!

[The guards seize the Fourth Man.]

LUSSURIOSO
Oh!

VINDICI
Alas, the duke is murder'd!

HIPPOLITO
And the nobles!

VINDICI
Surgeons, surgeons! Heart, does he breathe so long?

ANTONIO
A piteous tragedy, able to [make]
An old man's eyes bloodshot.

LUSSURIOSO
Oh!

VINDICI
Look to my lord the duke! [*Aside*] A vengeance throttle him!
[*To the Fourth Man*] Confess, thou murd'rous and [unhallowed] man,
Didst thou kill all these?

FOURTH MAN
None but the bastard I.

VINDICI
How came the duke slain then?

FOURTH MAN
We found him so.

LUSSURIOSO
Oh, villain!

VINDICI
Hark!

LUSSURIOSO
Those in the masque did murder us.

VINDICI
Law you now, sir.
Oh, marble impudence! Will you confess now?

FOURTH MAN
['Sblood], 'tis all false!

ANTONIO
Away with that foul monster,
Dipp'd in a prince's blood!

FOURTH MAN
Heart, 'tis a lie!

ANTONIO
Let him have bitter execution.

[Exit Fourth Man, guarded.]

VINDICI
[Aside] New marrow! No, I cannot be express'd!--
How fares my lord the duke?

LUSSURIOSO
Farewell to all;
He that climbs highest has the greatest fall.
My tongue is out of office.

VINDICI
Air, gentlemen, air!
[Whispering] Now thou'lt not prate on't, 'twas [Vindici] murd'red thee--

LUSSURIOSO
Oh!

VINDICI
Murd'red thy father--

LUSSURIOSO
Oh!

VINDICI
And I am he.
Tell nobody. *[Lussurioso dies.]* So, so, the duke's departed.

ANTONIO
It was a deadly hand that wounded him.
The rest, ambitious who should rule and sway,
After his death were so made all away.

VINDICI
My lord was unlikely.

HIPPOLITO
Now the hope
Of Italy lies in your reverend years.

VINDICI
Your hair will make the silver age again,
When there was fewer but more honest men.

ANTONIO
The burden's weighty and will press age down;
May I so rule that heaven [may] keep the crown.

VINDICI
The rape of your good lady has been quitted
With death on death.

ANTONIO
Just is the law above.
But of all things it puts me most to wonder
How the old duke came murd'red.

VINDICI
Oh, my lord!

ANTONIO
It was the strangeliest carried, I not [heard]
Of the like.

HIPPOLITO
'Twas all done for the best, my lord.

VINDICI
All for your grace's good; we may be bold to speak it now,
'Twas somewhat witty carried, tho' we say it.
'Twas we two murd'red him.

ANTONIO
You two?

VINDICI
None else, i'faith, my lord; nay, 'twas well manag'd.

ANTONIO
Lay hands upon those villains!

[Guards seize Vindici and Hippolito.]

VINDICI
How? On us?

ANTONIO
Bear 'em to speedy execution.

VINDICI
Heart, was't not for your good, my lord?

ANTONIO
My good! Away with 'em! Such an old man as he!
You that would murder him would murder me.

VINDICI
Is't come about?

HIPPOLITO
'Sfoot, brother, you begun.

VINDICI
May not we set as well as the duke's son?
Thou hast no conscience: are we not reveng'd?
Is there one enemy left alive amongst those?
'Tis time to die when we are ourselves our foes.
When murders shut deeds close, this curse does seal 'em:
If none disclose 'em they themselves reveal 'em!
This murder might have slept in tongueless brass
But for ourselves, and the world died an ass.
Now I remember too, here was Piato
Brought forth a knavish sentence: no doubt, said he,
But time will make the murderer bring forth himself.
'Tis well he died; he was a witch.
And now, my lord, since we are in forever,
This work was ours which else might have been slipp'd,
And if we list, we could have nobles clipp'd
And go for less than beggars, but we hate
To bleed so cowardly; we have enough. I'faith,
We're well: our mother turn'd, our sister true,
We die after a nest of dukes. Adieu.

Exeunt [Vindici and Hippolito, guarded].

ANTONIO
How subtly was that murder clos'd! Bear up
Those tragic bodies; 'tis a heavy season:
Pray heaven their blood may wash away all treason. *[Exeunt omnes.]*